²/₀₉

W9-BZP-903

DISCARDED

INTRODUCING ISSUES WITH OPPOSING VIEWPOINTS®

China

Lauri S. Friedman, *Book Editor*

GREENHAVEN PRESS
A part of Gale, Cengage Learning

GALE
CENGAGE Learning™

Detroit • New York • San Francisco • New Haven, Conn • Waterville, Maine • London

GALE
CENGAGE Learning

Christine Nasso, *Publisher*
Elizabeth Des Chenes, *Managing Editor*

For more information, contact:
Greenhaven Press
27500 Drake Rd.
Farmington Hills, MI 48331-3535
Or you can visit our Internet site at gale.cengage.com

For product information and technology assistance, contact us at

Gale Customer Support, 1-800-877-4253
For permission to use material from this text or product, submit all requests online at www.cengage.com/permissions

Further permissions questions can be emailed to permissionrequest@cengage.com

Articles in Greenhaven Press anthologies are often edited for length to meet page require-ments. In addition, original titles of these works are changed to clearly present the main thesis and to explicitly indicate the author's opinion. Every effort is made to ensure that Greenhaven Press accurately reflects the original intent of the authors. Every effort has been made to trace the owners of copyrighted material.

Cover image: Goh Chai Hin/AFP/Getty Images

LIBRARY OF CONGRESS CATALOGING-IN-PUBLICATION DATA

China / Lauri S. Friedman, book editor.
  p. cm. -- (Introducing issues with opposing viewpoints)
  Includes bibliographical references and index.
  ISBN 978-0-7377-4335-7 (hardcover)
  1. China--History--1976---Juvenile literature. 2. China--Social conditions--2000---Juvenile literature. 3. China--Economic conditions--2000---Juvenile literature. 4. United States--Foreign relations--China--Juvenile literature. 5. China--Foreign relations--United States--Juvenile literature. 6. Human rights--China--Juvenile literature. I. Friedman, Lauri S.
  DS779.2.C4419 2009
  951.06--dc22

                                                                        2009002469

Printed in the United States of America
1 2 3 4 5 6 7 13 12 11 10 09

Contents

Chapter 1

What Are the Most Serious Problems Facing China?

One of the major problems China faces is the pollution caused by new economic and industrial growth.

Google defended its decision to comply with the Chinese government's censorship policies by saying that even limited service expands access to information for Chinese users. A statement issued by the company after the google.cn controversy erupted said: "While removing search results is inconsistent with Google's mission, providing no information (or a heavily degraded user experience that amounts to no information) is more inconsistent with our mission."[5]

The extent to which the Internet is affecting social, cultural, economic, and political change in China is just one example of the way in which that nation is undergoing revolutionary change at lightning speed. China's complex relationship with the Internet is one of the many issues explored in *Introducing Issues with Opposing Viewpoints: China.* Readers will also consider arguments about China's relationship with the environment, its human rights record, and its problems with AIDS and democracy. Whether China is poised to be the next superpower, the extent to which it affects the U.S. economy, and its military ambitions are also explored. After examining these issues, readers can form their own opinions on what the future holds for China.

Notes

1. Clive Thompson, "Google's China Problem (and China's Google Problem)," *New York Times,* April 23, 2006. www.nytimes.com/2006/04/23/magazine/23google.html?ex=1303444800.
2. Christopher H. Smith, "The Internet in China: A Tool for Suppression?" Subcommittee on Global Human Rights, Africa, and International Operations, February 15, 2006.
3. Howard W. French, "Despite Flaws, Rights in China Have Expanded," *New York Times,* August 2, 2008. www.nytimes.com/2008/08/02/world/asia/02china.html?partner=rssnyt&emc=rss.
4. Quoted in French, "Despite Flaws, Rights in China Have Expanded."
5. Quoted in British Broadcasting Company, "Google Censors Itself for China," January 25, 2006. http://news.bbc.co.uk/2/hi/technology/4645596.stm.

thoughtfully and carefully. Useful charts, graphs, and cartoons supplement each article. A thorough introduction provides readers with crucial background on an issue. An annotated bibliography points the reader toward articles, books, and Web sites that contain additional information on the topic. An appendix of organizations to contact contains a wide variety of charities, nonprofit organizations, political groups, and private enterprises that each hold a position on the issue at hand. Finally, a comprehensive index allows readers to locate content quickly and efficiently.

Introducing Issues with Opposing Viewpoints is also significantly different from Opposing Viewpoints. As the series title implies, its presentation will help introduce students to the concept of opposing viewpoints and learn to use this material to aid in critical writing and debate. The series' four-color, accessible format makes the books attractive and inviting to readers of all levels. In addition, each viewpoint has been carefully edited to maximize a reader's understanding of the content. Short but thorough viewpoints capture the essence of an argument. A substantial, thought-provoking essay question placed at the end of each viewpoint asks the student to further investigate the issues raised in the viewpoint, compare and contrast two authors' arguments, or consider how one might go about forming an opinion on the topic at hand. Each viewpoint contains sidebars that include at-a-glance information and handy statistics. A Facts About section located in the back of the book further supplies students with relevant facts and figures.

Following in the tradition of the Opposing Viewpoints series, Greenhaven Press continues to provide readers with invaluable exposure to the controversial issues that shape our world. As John Stuart Mill once wrote: "The only way in which a human being can make some approach to knowing the whole of a subject is by hearing what can be said about it by persons of every variety of opinion and studying all modes in which it can be looked at by every character of mind. No wise man ever acquired his wisdom in any mode but this." It is to this principle that Introducing Issues with Opposing Viewpoints books are dedicated.

Foreword

I ndulging in a wide spectrum of ideas, beliefs, and perspectives is a critical cornerstone of democracy. After all, it is often debates over differences of opinion, such as whether to legalize abortion, how to treat prisoners, or when to enact the death penalty, that shape our society and drive it forward. Such diversity of thought is frequently regarded as the hallmark of a healthy and civilized culture. As the Reverend Clifford Schutjer of the First Congregational Church in Mansfield, Ohio, declared in a 2001 sermon, "Surrounding oneself with only like-minded people, restricting what we listen to or read only to what we find agreeable is irresponsible. Refusing to entertain doubts once we make up our minds is a subtle but deadly form of arrogance." With this advice in mind, Introducing Issues with Opposing Viewpoints books aim to open readers' minds to the critically divergent views that comprise our world's most important debates.

Introducing Issues with Opposing Viewpoints simplifies for students the enormous and often overwhelming mass of material now available via print and electronic media. Collected in every volume is an array of opinions that captures the essence of a particular controversy or topic. Introducing Issues with Opposing Viewpoints books embody the spirit of nineteenth-century journalist Charles A. Dana's axiom: "Fight for your opinions, but do not believe that they contain the whole truth, or the only truth." Absorbing such contrasting opinions teaches students to analyze the strength of an argument and compare it to its opposition. From this process readers can inform and strengthen their own opinions, or be exposed to new information that will change their minds. Introducing Issues with Opposing Viewpoints is a mosaic of different voices. The authors are statesmen, pundits, academics, journalists, corporations, and ordinary people who have felt compelled to share their experiences and ideas in a public forum. Their words have been collected from newspapers, journals, books, speeches, interviews, and the Internet, the fastest growing body of opinionated material in the world.

Introducing Issues with Opposing Viewpoints shares many of the well-known features of its critically acclaimed parent series, Opposing Viewpoints. The articles are presented in a pro/con format, allowing readers to absorb divergent perspectives side by side. Active reading questions preface each viewpoint, requiring the student to approach the material

Viewpoint

1

China Faces Serious Environmental Problems

Elizabeth C. Economy

"China's rapid development, often touted as an economic miracle, has become an environmental disaster."

In the following viewpoint Elizabeth C. Economy argues that runaway growth is leading China to the brink of environmental catastrophe. She explains that China's growing economy and booming population cause the country to consume resources at a fast and pollution-causing rate. Economy says that rapid development has dire consequences for the health, habitat, and well-being of China's people, as it exacts a heavy toll on the nation's resources and ecosystems. Making matters worse, environmental regulations in China are practically nonexistent. According to Economy, the warning signs of crisis are already obvious as buildings sink into the ground, environmental refugees seek shelter, and pollution-related death and sickness increase.

Economy is C.V. Start Senior Fellow and Director of Asia Studies at the Council on Foreign Relations. She is the author of *The River Runs Black: The Environmental Challenges to China's Future.*

Elizabeth C. Economy, "The Great Leap Backward?" *Foreign Affairs,* September/October 2007. Reproduced by permission of the publisher, www.foreignaffairs.org.

AS YOU READ, CONSIDER THE FOLLOWING QUESTIONS:
1. According to Economy, how many of the world's most polluted cities are in China?
2. What does the word *desertification* mean in the context of this viewpoint?
3. What percentage of water is lost due to leaky pipes in urban China, according to the author?

China's rapid development, often touted as an economic miracle, has become an environmental disaster. Record growth necessarily requires the gargantuan consumption of resources, but in China energy use has been especially unclean and inefficient, with dire consequences for the country's air, land, and water.

The coal that has powered China's economic growth, for example, is also choking its people. Coal provides about 70 percent of China's energy needs: the country consumed some 2.4 billion tons in 2006—more than the United States, Japan, and the United Kingdom combined. In 2000, China anticipated doubling its coal consumption by 2020; it is now expected to have done so by the end of this year. Consumption in China is huge partly because it is inefficient: as one Chinese official told *Der Spiegel* [a popular German magazine] in early 2006, "To produce goods worth $10,000 we need seven times the resources used by Japan, almost six times the resources used by the U.S. and—a particular source of embarrassment—almost three times the resources used by India."

Meanwhile, this reliance on coal is devastating China's environment. The country is home to 16 of the world's 20 most polluted cities, and four of the worst off among them are in the coal-rich province of Shanxi, in northeastern China. As much as 90 percent of China's sulfur dioxide emissions and 50 percent of its particulate emissions are the result of coal use. Particulates are responsible for respiratory problems among the population, and acid rain, which is caused by sulfur dioxide emissions, falls on one-quarter of China's territory and on one-third of its agricultural land, diminishing agricultural output and eroding buildings.

A Booming Population

Yet coal use may soon be the least of China's air-quality problems. The transportation boom poses a growing challenge to China's air quality. Chinese developers are laying more than 52,700 miles of new highways throughout the country. Some 14,000 new cars hit China's roads each day. By 2020, China is expected to have 130 million cars, and by 2050—or perhaps as early as 2040—it is expected to have even more cars than the United States. Beijing already pays a high price for this boom. In a 2006 survey, Chinese respondents

Fourteen thousand new cars hit the road in China every day, posing a major problem for China's air quality.

rated Beijing the 15th most livable city in China, down from the 4th in 2005, with the drop due largely to increased traffic and pollution. Levels of airborne particulates are now six times higher in Beijing than in New York City.

China's grand-scale urbanization plans will aggravate matters. China's leaders plan to relocate 400 million people—equivalent to well over the entire population of the United States—to newly developed urban centers between 2000 and 2030. In the process, they will erect half of all the buildings expected to be constructed in the world during that period. This is a troubling prospect considering that Chinese buildings are not energy efficient—in fact, they are roughly two and a half times less so than those in Germany. Furthermore, newly urbanized Chinese, who use air conditioners, televisions, and refrigerators, consume about three and a half times more energy than do their rural counterparts. And although China is one of the world's largest producers of solar cells, compact fluorescent lights, and energy-efficient windows, these are produced mostly for export. Unless more of these energy-saving goods stay at home, the building boom will result in skyrocketing energy consumption and pollution.

China's land has also suffered from unfettered development and environmental neglect. Centuries of deforestation, along with the overgrazing of grasslands and overcultivation of cropland, have left much of China's north and northwest seriously degraded. In the past half century, moreover, forests and farmland have had to make way for industry and sprawling cities, resulting in diminishing crop yields, a loss in biodiversity, and local climatic change. The Gobi Desert, which now engulfs much of western and northern China, is spreading by about 1,900 square miles annually; some reports say that despite Beijing's aggressive reforestation efforts, one-quarter of the entire country is now desert. China's State Forestry Administration estimates that desertification has hurt some 400 million Chinese, turning tens of millions of them into environmental refugees, in search of new homes and jobs. Meanwhile, much of China's arable soil is contaminated, raising concerns about food safety. As much as ten percent of China's farmland is believed to be polluted, and every year 12 million tons of grain are contaminated with heavy metals absorbed from the soil.

The Reckless Use of Water

And then there is the problem of access to clean water. Although China holds the fourth-largest freshwater resources in the world (after Brazil, Russia, and Canada), skyrocketing demand, overuse, inefficiencies, pollution, and unequal distribution have produced a situation in which two-thirds of China's approximately 660 cities have less water than they need and 110 of them suffer severe shortages. According to Ma Jun, a leading Chinese water expert, several cities near Beijing and Tianjin, in the northeastern region of the country, could run out of water in five to seven years.

Growing demand is part of the problem, of course, but so is enormous waste. The agricultural sector lays claim to 66 percent of the water China consumes, mostly for irrigation, and manages to waste more than half of that. Chinese industries are highly inefficient: they generally use 10–20 percent more water than do their counterparts in developed countries. Urban China is an especially huge squanderer: it loses up to 20 percent of the water it consumes through leaky pipes—a problem that China's Ministry of Construction has pledged to address in the next two to three years. As urbanization proceeds and incomes rise, the Chinese, much like people in Europe and the United States, have become larger consumers of water: they take lengthy showers, use washing machines and dishwashers, and purchase second homes with lawns that need to be watered. Water consumption in Chinese cities jumped by 6.6 percent during 2004–5. China's plundering of its ground-water reserves, which has created massive underground tunnels, is causing a corollary problem: some of China's wealthiest cities are sinking—in the case of Shanghai and Tianjin, by more than six feet during the past decade and a half. In Beijing, subsidence has destroyed factories, buildings, and underground pipelines and is threatening the city's main international airport.

> # FAST FACT
>
> According to *National Geographic*, China has doubled its consumption of coal since 1990, adding the equivalent of two coal-fired power plants each week— a capacity comparable to the entire power grid of the United Kingdom each year.

Water Pollution in China

About half of China's population lives in areas where demand for water exceeds its supply, and what water is available is tainted. For example, about 50 percent of the Yellow River's water is undrinkable as a result of pollution.

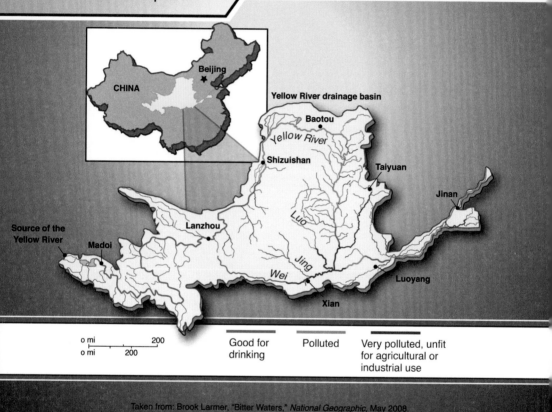

Beijing

CHINA

Yellow River drainage basin

Baotou

Yellow River

Shizuishan

Taiyuan

Jinan

Source of the Yellow River

Madoi

Lanzhou

Luo

Jing

Wei

Luoyang

Xian

o mi 200
o mi 200

Good for drinking

Polluted

Very polluted, unfit for agricultural or industrial use

Taken from: Brook Larmer, "Bitter Waters," *National Geographic*, May 2008.

Pollution is also endangering China's water supplies. China's ground water, which provides 70 percent of the country's total drinking water, is under threat from a variety of sources, such as polluted surface water, hazardous waste sites, and pesticides and fertilizers. According to one report by the government-run Xinhua News Agency, the aquifers in 90 percent of Chinese cities are polluted. More than 75 percent of the river water flowing through China's urban areas is considered unsuitable for drinking or fishing, and

Christopher H. Smith, chairman of the U.S. House of Representatives subcommittee that oversees global human rights, spoke for many when he called google.cn nothing more than "a megaphone for communist propaganda and a tool for controlling public opinion."[2] Smith and others argue that China may be active online, but thanks to google.cn, its citizens are not any freer because of it.

Interestingly, public opinion surveys of Chinese citizens have found they do not necessarily mind their government's censorship of the Internet. In fact, a poll conducted by the Pew Internet & American Life Project from 2000–2007 found that a whopping 85 percent think the Internet should be controlled in some way by the government. Overwhelming majorities prefer that online censors be responsible for controlling pornography, violent content, and spam (87, 86, and 83 percent, respectively). Such high support for government censorship of the Internet may well be a symptom of the problem rather than a reflection of the people's true desires, but it seems clear that most Chinese Internet users are happy to be online at all. And greater access to information has helped them improve their living conditions and win more rights, as reported by journalist Howard W. French: "Homeowners in cities like Shanghai and Chongqing have [used the Internet to resist] government development schemes with some success, and the proliferation of petitioners with all kinds of grievances presents the authorities with an informal check on their power."[3]

Another example of how a censored Internet is managing to help empower the masses comes from Guizhou Province, where the mysterious death of a teenage girl in June 2008 prompted rumors that spread on the Internet of a police cover-up. The online information eventually led to a huge public rally to demand a new investigation into the girl's death. The rally turned violent, with Chinese authorities firing rubber bullets and beating young protesters. State-run news agencies reported that the rally was peaceful, but their false reports were quickly exposed by videos of the rally that were uploaded to YouTube. Said Wu Hanpin, who took pictures of the riot and posted them on his blog, "I saw a gap between the official story and the reality, which was mind-blowing."[4] Although his blog was shut down by censors in just four days, it was online long enough for hundreds of thousands of people to register on it.

These mixed success stories could be seen as vindicating Google's rationale for entering the Chinese market in the first place. Indeed,

Introduction

Napoleon Bonaparte once famously called China a sleeping giant, advising other nations to "let him sleep. For when he wakes he will move the world." The twenty-first century has seen the Chinese giant slowly waking to numerous cultural, social, political, and economic changes, many of which have been heralded by the Internet. Indeed, China made headlines in 2008 when it surpassed the United States as the nation with the highest number of Internet users in the world. More than 250 million people in China now use the Internet—more than the populations of Argentina, Germany, Iran, and Italy combined. China's growing Internet use has brought significant change to the country and yet has also been used by officials to continue the Communist Party's reign of censorship and oppression.

Dubbed the "Great Firewall of China," the Chinese Internet is among just a handful in the world that are significantly censored by government officials. The issue of Chinese Internet censorship was brought to the forefront in 2006, when the popular search engine Google launched service there that complied with the nation's censorship policies. Google.cn blocks many Web sites that criticize the Chinese government and discuss taboo subjects like teen pregnancy, religion, homosexuality, and even dating. Other censored sites include those that cover touchy political issues such as the 1989 massacre in Tiananmen Square. Censored search results are delivered with the tagline, "In accordance with local laws, regulations and policies, part of the search result is not shown." Explains *New York Times* reporter Clive Thompson, "If you search for 'Tibet' or 'Falun Gong' [a religious group banned in China] most anywhere in the world on google.com, you'll find thousands of blog entries, news items and chat rooms on Chinese repression. Do the same search inside China on google.cn, and most, if not all, of these links will be gone. Google will have erased them completely."[1]

Google was roundly criticized for complying with China's censorship laws. Some called the decision to help the Chinese government with its censorship efforts a violation of Google's mission statement to "Do No Evil" and a violation of American ethics. Representative

Viewpoint

2

China Is Taking Steps to Solve Its Environmental Problems

"China's central government has stepped up its commitment to the environment and resource conservation."

Yingling Liu

In the following viewpoint Yingling Liu argues that China's government is adequately addressing its environmental problems. She says that although China's two-decades-long surge of economic growth has impacted the environment, related concerns are now topping the nation's agenda. Liu explains that China's governing agencies are enforcing new environmental standards, its industries are adhering to them, and its people are becoming more environmentally conscious. These developments have resulted in energy efficiency and a decline in emissions. China has been so successful, in fact, that its new technologies and industrial controls are now on levels that match or surpass Europe, the United States, and Japan. Furthermore, Liu argues that China leads the world in its development of "green technologies" and renewable energy sources such as solar and

Yingling Liu, "China's Coming Environmental Renaissance," worldwatch.org, November 29, 2007. Copyright © 2008 Worldwatch Institute. Reproduced by permission.

wind power. For all of these reasons, she concludes that China will be a key asset in solving the world's environmental problems.

Liu is the manager of the China Program at the Worldwatch Institute. She is a graduate of Yale University and Beijing Normal University.

AS YOU READ, CONSIDER THE FOLLOWING QUESTIONS:
1. According to Liu, what recent law has tightened China's auto emission and fuel economy standards?
2. What percentage did China's "energy intensity" drop between 1995 and 2004? What bearing does this have on the author's argument?
3. How many factories were closed in the city of Wuxi because they were dumping waste into Tai Lake?

As a Chinese citizen and researcher who has followed [China's environmental] developments for many years, I am . . . optimistic that China is beginning to turn the corner on its monumental environmental challenges. . . .

From the start of this millennium, China's central government has stepped up its commitment to the environment and resource conservation. The country's top leaders have changed their rhetoric, no longer stating that economic growth is the paramount priority. Instead, they are giving equal weighting to the environment and resource conservation. They have not only set ambitious targets for energy savings and pollution control, but they have labeled these efforts as two paramount tasks for the government. Meeting these goals will naturally take time. It took nearly three decades after [former Communist Party leader Deng Xiaoping's] economic reforms for China to get where it is today. It will similarly take more than a few years for the country to achieve its goal of achieving a harmonious and sustainable economy.

New Environmental Laws Are Working

Changes have already taken place. Growing political determination has begun to translate into legislation and macro-level indus-

trial restructuring as well as into the empowerment of key government administrative agencies. Environmental improvement has been granted a central role in the 11th Five-Year Plan, and a new Environmental Impact Assessment Law recently entered into force. China now boasts auto emissions standards that are comparable to the European level, fuel economy standards that exceed those in the United States, and a national renewable energy law that has proven far more effective than any similar legislation passed by the U.S. Congress to date. However imperfect some of these laws may be—and no government policies are ever perfect—it is clear that environmental policy is advancing rapidly in China and that the nation's leaders are working hard to learn from the successes and failures of other countries.

China's top economic planning body, the National Development and Reform Commission (NDRC), is taking action to adjust the country's industrial structure, aiming for more balance and less energy use and pollution. It has mandated the shutdown of thousands of small, inefficient coal-fired power plants and heavily polluting industrial furnaces and boilers in favor of larger, more efficient plants. The ruling is being implemented effectively nationwide. Energy efficiency is advancing with the adoption of new technologies and the development of less energy-intensive light industries and services. China's energy intensity (the

FAST FACT

According to Foreign Policy in Focus, China has just 22 vehicles per 1,000 people, while the United States has 764 vehicles per 1,000 people.

amount of energy required to produce one yuan [basic unit of Chinese currency] of national income) fell by 30 percent between 1995 and 2004. Without this improvement, the nation's energy consumption would be 30 percent higher today—equivalent to Japan's total energy use.

Industrial Polluters Are Regulated

It is true that China has failed to achieve targets for energy savings and pollution control set at the beginning of the millennium. Premier

Wen Jiabao acknowledged and criticized this failure early this year [2007] in his annual report to the National People's Congress, the equivalent of a U.S. *State of the Union* speech. The unprecedented public acknowledgement from the state head sent another unmistakable message to unyielding industry leaders and local governments, who had become used to the environmental inertia accumulated during the two-decade-long rush for economic development.

Chinese premier Wen Jiabao, in his annual report to the National People's Congress, said the government plans to work harder to achieve its target for pollution controls.

In the first half of 2007, the reduction in China's energy intensity accelerated, dropping to 2.8 percent below the same period the previous year, due mainly to industrial efficiency improvements. These achievements gave the central government renewed confidence to propose specific targets for energy conservation and pollution control in China's national climate change action plan, released in June [2007], which will likely provide the framework for the country's stance in future climate change negotiations.

The country's environmental agency is also being strengthened. SEPA [Chinese State Environmental Protection Administration] has gained significant power in recent years and has shaken off its moniker as a "rubber stamp" agency. In 2005 and 2006, it launched several rounds of crackdowns against giant industrial polluters. And early this year [2007], it issued a strong measure that suspends or restricts the environmental impact assessment permitting process for certain construction projects until the companies comply with pollution regulations. The agency is also partnering with the Ministry of Supervision on environmental investigation, the People's Bank of China, and the China Banking Regulatory Commission on initiating a "green banking" mechanism, and plans to work with other ministries and departments on regulating polluters.

Change Is Occurring at Local Levels

[Critics blame] much of China's pollution on local officials who have few incentives to prioritize environmental protection. This is beginning to change. The city of Wuxi recently responded to the toxic pollution coming out of local water taps by ordering the closure of 1,340 factories that were dumping their effluent into Tai Lake. They did this because outraged citizens had begun protesting strenuously, presenting significant risk to the careers of local officials. Of course, those polluting factories had been supported by those same officials in order to meet the demands for jobs and growth. But a newly awakened Chinese populace is now realizing that a growing economy isn't worth much if the air and water are poisoned as a result.

The combination of grassroots revolt and political pressure from Beijing is clearly having an impact on local and provincial governments. Increasing numbers of officials, including in Guangdong,

Chongqing, and Shandong provinces, are working hard or vowing to promote the concept of "greener development." The deeper challenge facing China's governmental bodies is similar to that in much of the developing world and also in the United States: economic development and environmental progress are often at loggerheads, and continued vigilance is required to ensure that the environment does not lose out as a result. The stakes are simply higher in China, due to the scale of ecological problems and the intensity of the modern Chinese economy. . . .

Technological Innovation Is Key

In addition to political reform, technological innovation holds equal, if not greater, weight in China's ability to reverse its environmental situation. The country has already taken the lead in adopting many green technologies, particularly in the area of renewable energy. It is now the world's largest market for solar hot water systems and is home to nearly two-thirds of global capacity. More than 10 percent of Chinese households now bathe in water heated by vacuum tube solar collectors, rather than the large gas or electric water heaters found in most U.S. suburban homes. The International Energy Agency reports that in 2005, China saved nearly 14 million tons of carbon dioxide emissions through its use of solar heating systems. Vast "forests" of the units are jostling for space on the rooftops of entire neighborhoods in cities like Rizhao and Kunming. The devices are easy to manufacture, and costs have fallen dramatically as the technology matures and competition thrives in a freer market.

Wind power, meanwhile, is now the fastest growing power-generation technology in China, with existing capacity doubling during 2006 alone. Although China was only number five in added capacity behind Germany, Spain, the United States, and India, the potential for further expansion and cost reduction is huge. China's solar PV [photovoltaics] industry has literally developed from scratch into a dynamic, globally competitive sector within five years, driven by ever-rising global demand and resulting in the creation of several world-leading manufacturers and a group of new billionaires. Although most of China's solar cells are currently exported, as Chinese companies succeed in driving down costs, they will no doubt find their way into

the huge domestic market. Similar technological advances could have dramatic implications in dealing with wastewater, solid waste, and the energy efficiency of China's buildings.

With its expanding industrial base, increasingly skilled labor force, and geared-up R & D [research and development] efforts, China brings hope—not despair—for a global leap forward in environmental stewardship.

EVALUATING THE AUTHORS' ARGUMENTS:

In this viewpoint Yingling Liu claims that China's auto emission standards are comparable to the European level and that China's fuel economy standards exceed those in the United States. How do you think Elizabeth C. Economy, the author of the previous viewpoint, would respond to this argument? Explain your answer using evidence from the texts.

China Is Facing an Energy Crisis

Peter Aldhous

"The most immediate problem for China is that its economic growth is already outstripping its energy supplies."

In the following viewpoint Peter Aldhous argues that China is facing an energy crisis. He explains that China's massive economic growth has come as a result of overusing coal, a dirty energy source that China is running out of. Aldhous points out that blackouts in many regions are visible proof that coal cannot meet current demand. The author discusses the human cost of coal, both in the mining operations and in airborne particulate-related deaths. According to Aldhous, in the next ten years the Chinese economy will grow fourfold and China's energy demand will double. If the status quo continues, Aldhous argues that coal cannot possibly meet the oncoming demand without throwing China into environmental, social, and international crisis.

Aldhous is *Nature*'s chief news and features editor.

AS YOU READ, CONSIDER THE FOLLOWING QUESTIONS:
1. How many of China's thirty-one provinces and municipalities have lacked sufficient power?

2. According to the author, what percentage of China's electricity is generated by burning coal?
3. With what country does Aldhous claim China, if dependent on oil imports, could face major conflict?

China is booming, and its hunger for energy is insatiable. For its people, the dismal air quality across much of the country is a constant reminder of its reliance on coal and other dirty fuels. When *Nature* visited Beijing to meet the technocrats responsible for China's energy policy, the city was blanketed in acrid smog. After just a few days of stagnant weather, visibility in some districts had dropped to tens of metres. Flights were delayed and the Beijing Environmental Protection Agency advised people to stay indoors. You could almost taste the sulphur in the air.

Straining to Meet Demand

Energy and its consequences for health and the environment are high on the Chinese political agenda. But the hard-headed approach of the country's leaders should give us all pause for thought. China's energy policy will continue to be based around coal, they say, so the question of whether this notoriously filthy fuel can ever be made 'clean' is central to the country's development—and to the long-term stability of the global climate.

The most immediate problem for China is that its economic growth is already outstripping its energy supplies. In boomtowns from Shenzhen to Chengdu, electricity is now an unstable commodity. [In 2004,] 24 of China's 31 provinces, municipalities and autonomous regions admitted that they lacked sufficient power. In the summer when drought curtails hydropower and air conditioners surge into life, blackouts have become commonplace.

> **FAST FACT**
>
> According to the International Energy Agency, China will become the world's top consumer of energy, surpassing the United States, between 2010 and 2012.

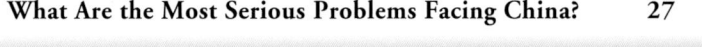

Barges of coal are transported on the Grand Canal in China. China's growth has resulted in an overuse of coal and has had a detrimental effect on the environment.

The nation's coal mines are straining to meet the demand, at a terrible human cost. According to conservative official estimates, more than 6,000 workers were killed in China's mines [in 2004]—making them the world's most dangerous—and the death rate was undiminished in the first half of 2005.

Most coal-related fatalities never make the headlines, however. Many Chinese cities fail to meet international—or even their own—standards for air quality, causing hundreds of thousands of premature deaths each year. China's increasing use of coal is also sending CO_2 emissions skyrocketing, threatening a global climate disaster. "We understand that coal means not only energy, but also social and environmental impacts in the long term," says Zhou Dadi, director-general of the Energy Research Institute in Beijing and a leading adviser on energy strategy to China's leaders.

An Insatiable Appetite for Coal

While Dadi and other senior energy planners recognize these problems, their enthusiasm for coal remains strong. The country's leaders are determined that its economy will quadruple in size by 2020, which will require at least a doubling of the energy supply. Coal will bear most of the burden. "We have to increase coal consumption" says Guo Yuan, an energy systems analyst at Dadi's institute. "It's not a good picture, but we have to do it."

Electricity generation is by far the biggest consumer of energy, although the demands of the transport sector are growing fast. Between 75% and 80% of China's electricity is generated by burning coal. Another 20% comes from large-scale hydropower projects, with most of the rest coming from nuclear stations. As yet, oil, natural gas and renewables such as wind barely feature in the electricity mix. But by 2020, according to official projections, gas-fired stations could be meeting 15% of China's electricity needs, while nuclear power may have expanded to around 5%. And thanks to a law passed in February [2005] designed to promote renewable energy, wind and other renewables could account for 10%. However, with power demands poised

" FIRST WE'LL VACATION AT THE SHORE, THEN WE'LL GO TO THE MOUNTAINS, THEN UP TO THE LAKE..... "

to double over the same period, it's clear that a massive increase in coal consumption is unavoidable.

An Uncertain Future

Sustaining economic growth is the leadership's priority, say seasoned China watchers, but it wants to achieve this without compromising energy security. China lacks substantial reserves of oil and natural gas, and is determined not to become heavily dependent on imports. But the country has coal in abundance. So it will use the fuel in ever-larger quantities, mainly to avoid a reliance on Russian oil and gas that could eventually bring the two powers to the brink of war.

But can China meet its energy needs without poisoning its environment and filling the lungs of millions of people with particulates and oxides of sulphur and nitrogen? The effects of acid rain are spreading, and there are suggestions that soot is already disrupting the regional climate.

EVALUATING THE AUTHORS' ARGUMENTS:

In the viewpoint you just read, Peter Aldhous discusses China's reliance on coal, critiquing not only coal's ability to meet future demands, but also coal's contribution to global warming. How do you think Steve Howard and Changhua Wu, the authors of the next viewpoint, would respond to this argument? Explain your answer using evidence from the text.

China Is Taking Steps to Thwart an Energy Crisis

Steve Howard and Changhua Wu

"China is already the leading renewable energy producer . . . with the largest hydro-electric fleet and fifth largest wind power fleet in the world."

In the following viewpoint Steve Howard and Changhua Wu argue that China is successfully taking steps to avert an energy crisis. They discuss how China's vast population and enormous economy have made it one of the world's largest contributors of carbon emissions, a global warming instigator. But recently, China's carbon status has changed. The authors explain how China's focus on developing a low-carbon economy has resulted in lower carbon emissions and less coal use. Furthermore, they call China a world leader in renewable energy technology and say these developments will only further stimulate China's economic growth as these technologies are manufactured and exported globally. Howard and Wu conclude that the tides have changed—although China was once touted as a major environmental villain, it will now lead the world toward a sustainable energy future.

Steve Howard and Changhua Wu, "China's Clean Revolution," The Climate Group, July 31, 2008. Reproduced by permission.

Howard is founder and CEO of the Climate Group. Wu lives in Beijing and leads the Climate Group's strategic developments and operations in China.

AS YOU READ, CONSIDER THE FOLLOWING QUESTIONS:
  1. What global ranking does China have for investment in renewable technologies, as reported by the authors?
  2. What do the authors say the Global Wind Council announced in 2008?
  3. In 2007 how many electric bicycles were sold in China? In the same year, how many energy-efficient cars were sold?

It has been widely reported in the media that China has become the largest national emitter of carbon dioxide (CO_2), a potent global warming gas, and that the country is and will continue to be one of the most important players in finding a solution to the climate change challenge. Scientists have pointed out that in the period before 2002, when over 90% of human carbon emissions were released, China accounted for only 7% of the global total, compared to 26% and 29% for the European Union and United States respectively. But since the turn of the century, the proportion of emissions from China has been growing steadily and it now accounts for over 24% of the annual total, a figure which is growing every year.

Although China has a population over 1.3 billion people, CO_2 emissions per person are relatively low. If China's citizens emitted as much CO_2 as America's, China's total emissions would be roughly equivalent to those of the entire planet today. A recent report by Sir Nicholas Stern and the London School of Economics proposed a target of two metric tons of CO_2 per person per year for all countries by 2050. From this perspective, while China's carbon intensity per person is barely above the world average, it is still far above where it needs to be by mid-century. . . .

Investments in Renewables Are Growing Quickly

According to the *Renewables 2007 Global Status Report,* China is already the leading renewable energy producer in terms of installed generating capacity, with the largest hydro-electric fleet and fifth largest wind power fleet in the world. China plans to almost double the proportion of renewable energy it uses from 8% in 2006 to 15% in 2020, with concrete targets for hydro power capacity at 300 Gigawatts (GW), bioenergy power at 30 GW, wind power at 30 GW, and solar power at 1.8 GW. The country's renewable energy targets are close behind those of the most advanced countries such as those of the European Union which have set a renewable energy target of 20% by 2020.

China ranked second for the absolute dollar amount invested in renewable energy in 2007 with over US$12 billion, trailing the leader Germany which invested US$14 billion. The nominal sizes of the Chinese and German economies were almost equal at US$3.3 trillion in 2007, meaning that China trails leader Germany only slightly in renewable energy investment as a percentage of GDP [gross domestic product]. New Energy Finance predicts that another US$398 billion of investment is needed to reach China's 2020 renewable energy goals, or an average of US$33 billion per year mainly for wind, biomass, hydro and solar installations.

The Top Manufacturer of Solar and Wind Technologies

China is currently a leading manufacturer of solar photovoltaic technology, with 820 Megawatts of production by the end of 2007, second only to Japan. The country is set to capitalise on this growing export opportunity as the world transitions to a low carbon future.

In addition to China's own local wind power installations which grew by around 120% in 2007, the Global Wind Energy Council announced in early 2008 that China will become the world's leading manufacturer of wind turbines by 2009.

China is also competing for or taking the lead in the production of other critical renewable and low carbon technologies such as solar water heaters (holding 60% of the global market), energy efficient home appliances and rechargeable batteries.

Pioneering Efforts in Fuel Efficiency

Beyond its traditional reliance on bicycles and public transport, China is now introducing measures to limit oil consumption from its growing motor vehicle fleet, implementing fuel efficiency standards for cars 40% higher than those in the USA, although still lagging behind those in

Workers install photovoltaic cells at a hotel in Baoding, China. China is the leading manufacturer of photovoltaic technology in the world.

Europe and Japan. China has also succeeded in scaling up a range of low carbon transport technologies; over 21 million electric bicycles and 1.64 million energy efficient compact cars were sold in 2007, and domestic hybrid and electric vehicle technologies are progressing rapidly.

Biofuels also feature strongly, with China being the third largest ethanol producer in the world. The country has begun converting an area of marginal land half the size of the United Kingdom into biofuel forests, hopefully easing the competition between biofuels and grain crops that has contributed to food price increases. There are plans to produce 12 million metric tons of low carbon fuel per year by 2020.

Curbing Carbon Emissions

The energy intensity of the Chinese economy has dropped by over 60% since 1980. Moreover, China has targeted a further 20% reduction between 2006 and 2010.

Fossil fuels still provide 80% of China's power, but by replacing small and inefficient power stations with high efficiency super-critical technology, China hopes to avoid approximately 37.6 million metric tons of CO_2 emissions every year.

The Chinese Government has also put in place an ambitious monitoring, benchmarking and control system for China's 1,000 largest energy consuming companies, between them responsible for 33% of national energy usage. The programme stipulates that these companies must reduce their energy intensity to accomplish an overall energy saving of 100 million metric ton standard coal equivalent (over 833 million Megawatt-hours) by 2010.

A Low Carbon Framework Is in Place

In addition to the overarching 20% energy intensity reduction target and the 15% renewable energy target, a comprehensive set of complementary regulations have been developed covering almost every sector of China's economy.

Fuel economy standards were issued in 2005; one of the world's most comprehensive mandatory energy efficiency testing and labelling standards for home appliances was implemented the same year; a tax of up to 20% on gas guzzling SUVs [sport utility vehicles] was introduced in 2006 while compact cars are only taxed at 3%; strict building efficiency design codes have been introduced which will cut energy consumption of new buildings by 50%; and China's Renewable Energy Law, which also came into effect in 2006, mandates that the power grid purchase renewable power, giving subsidies for wind and biopower projects.

> **FAST FACT**
>
> China's government has pledged to make renewable energy account for 15 percent of the country's energy needs by 2020. It also has pledged to cut coal use by 13 percent by that year.

Riding a Low Carbon Wave

A low carbon wave has swept up literally tens of thousands of Chinese companies into new markets and created some of China's most successful business leaders. For example, China's six largest solar photovoltaics (PV) manufacturers, most of which did not exist 10 years ago, had a total market value of over US$15 billion by July 2008. Some other rapidly growing areas are: the solar water heater market, which employs over 600,000 people in China, is worth over US$2 billion per year and is growing at 20% annually; the energy efficient

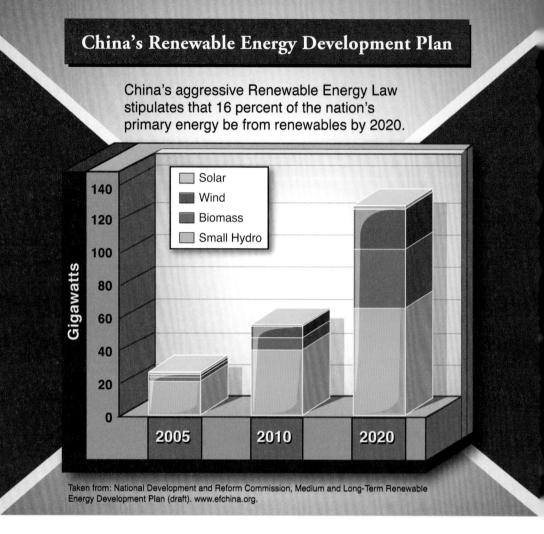

China's Renewable Energy Development Plan

China's aggressive Renewable Energy Law stipulates that 16 percent of the nation's primary energy be from renewables by 2020.

Legend:
- Solar
- Wind
- Biomass
- Small Hydro

Y-axis: Gigawatts (0, 20, 40, 60, 80, 100, 120, 140)
X-axis: 2005, 2010, 2020

Taken from: National Development and Reform Commission, Medium and Long-Term Renewable Energy Development Plan (draft). www.efchina.org.

compact car market, which was worth over US$50 billion in 2007; the electric bicycle market, which was worth over US$6 billion in 2007; and China's leading wind turbine manufacturer, which has a rapidly rising market value of over US$6 billion.

Across power, efficiency and transport, China has frequently taken the route followed by most countries focusing policies on new buildings, factories, vehicles or products, instead of replacing or retrofitting old ones, which is a more complicated and expensive approach. For this reason it will take several years to see the full effect of the initiatives which have been introduced. Many opportunities still exist for China to further speed up the phase out of older technologies.

Another qualifying factor, when considering the data presented in this report, is level of implementation. It is inevitable that some companies will evade the system. However China's clear improvement in energy intensity to this point indicates that it has been as successful in overcoming resistance to new efficiency policies as any country. For example, China's energy intensity has recently shown two consecutive drops, of 1.79% in 2006 and 3.66% in 2007. As more Chinese companies and products begin to comply with the new regulation, China will face the continuing challenge of monitoring and ensuring compliance, encouraging innovation and continually pushing up standards to best-available technology.

Fuel-Efficient Technologies Spur Economic Growth

With companies fielding strong investment, reaping impressive profits and seeing double or even triple digit growth in low carbon sectors, China and its new generation of low carbon entrepreneurs are already seeing significant economic benefits as a result of their push into the low carbon economy.

[In 2007] The Climate Group's *In The Black* report documented how, even in the absence of consistent policy, the low carbon economy is booming in four major industrialised countries. What this latest report shows is that this is not just a niche market for rich countries, but rather that—with their cost advantages and abundant abatement opportunities—investment in low carbon solutions can be equally, if not more profitable, job-creating and socially beneficial in developing nations.

China in particular has embraced this opportunity, once again showing that moving to a low carbon economy is consistent with growth, development and energy security objectives.

EVALUATING THE AUTHORS' ARGUMENTS:

This viewpoint by Steve Howard and Changhua Wu is part of a report published by the Climate Group. What is the Climate Group, and who are its major supporters? Does knowing who sponsors the Climate Group influence your opinion of Howard and Wu's arguments? Why or why not?

Viewpoint 5

China Is Facing a Population Crisis

Rachel Nowak

"The one-child policy and a cultural preference for boys has driven many parents to opt for sex-selective abortion, creating . . . a huge deficit of girls."

In the following viewpoint Rachel Nowak argues that China is facing a population crisis. Nowak explains that for decades China has embedded "social engineering" into its economic policies. For example, in the 1950s large families were promoted as part of China's economic growth. Then in the 1970s, China's population doubled, and rigid incentives, such as a law allowing just one child per couple, were enacted to counter the population explosion. With the one-child policy still in place, Nowak says a demographic and economic crisis is pending. She warns that the younger, less-populous generation will be overburdened in caring for China's current aging work fleet and in sustaining China's colossal economy. Furthermore, China's population policies have caused more boys to be born than girls, which is also a population crisis in the making. For all of these reasons, Nowak concludes that China needs to rework its policies before it experiences severe demographic, social, and economic turmoil.

Nowak is *New Scientist*'s biology features editor and Australian editor.

AS YOU READ, CONSIDER THE FOLLOWING QUESTIONS:
1. According to the article, what percentage of China's population is currently of working age?
2. According to Nowak, China has ten people of working age for each person over sixty-five. How is this ratio expected to change in the next three decades?
3. How many fewer women than men, ages twenty to forty-nine, does Nowak speculate there will be by the year 2025? By the year 2050?

It has been called the demographic sweet spot—a huge working-age population supporting a relatively small number of old and young people—and it has helped power China's economic explosion. China hit that sweet spot because of decades of social engineering. In the late 1950s, Mao Zedong [Chinese leader, 1949–1976] promoted large families to power his economic vision of a Great Leap Forward, and by 1976 the population had almost doubled. This prompted the introduction of national family planning policies to restrict the number of children a couple could have. With some modifications, these policies are still in place. They were designed to put a brake on runaway population growth, end poverty and encourage economic development. In part, the plan has worked: today almost 72 per cent of Chinese people are of working age.

But the country's drive to reduce birthrates—known outside China as the one-child policy—might have sown the seeds of a massive demographic pile-up. When today's parents are old, how will their children support them?

An Aging Workforce

Something similar is happening in parts of Europe and Asia, where falling birthrates are raising the average age of the population. In China, though, this change will be especially dramatic. In a paper to be published [November 2007] Wolfgang Lutz, a demographer at the International Institute for Applied Systems Analysis in Laxenburg, Austria, predicts that the ratio of over-65s to 15-to-65-year-olds in China will increase almost threefold between 2010 and 2035. That means for each person over 65 there will be just three working-age people, compared to 10 today.

So should China relax or abandon the one-child policy to avoid an impending demographic crisis? Some demographers say that if it doesn't the country risks an economic crash. Others argue that the policy should stay in place to prevent the already huge population outgrowing available resources. Ultimately, however, making any kind of decision comes down to knowing how many people there are in China already and how many babies are being born each year. Because of the country's social engineering policies, that's trickier than it sounds.

Hidden Births Skew Population Estimates

The so-called one-child policy is actually a raft of regional regulations with many exemptions. In some regions certain ethnic minorities are not included, for example, and remarried couples can have a child together even if they have children from a previous relationship. In fact only about a third of people of reproductive age are limited to one child. The regulations are enforced with varying degrees of rigour in different regions. Public education is widely used to instruct couples on the benefits of having just one child, and in some places there are fines and other penalties for having too many children. In the early days, women having more than one child in the strictest areas faced forced sterilisation or abortion—practices that are now banned.

Despite the penalties there are good reasons to flout the rules. Though the government has recently set up a state pension scheme, most people in rural areas assume they will be dependent on their children—and most importantly their sons—to provide for them during their old age. So often couples opt not to register births, especially when the firstborn is female.

The total number of these "missing babies" is unknown, and that has led to huge discrepancies in birthrate estimates. Of . . . 30 or so . . . published estimates for 2000, the Chinese national census is the lowest, at 1.22 children per woman. This is way below replacement levels and is believed by virtually no one. Other estimates put the figure at up to 2.3 children using various criteria to correct for the missing

Experts argue that in the coming decades, China's one-child policy will cause workforce and other population problems if the policy is not adjusted.

babies. The National Population and Family Planning Commission of China assumes a birthrate of 1.8, a figure that some demographers believe is a dangerous overestimation which could make the government complacent. "Every national population survey indicates that it is lower than 1.6, and most scholars believe it is between 1.6 and 1.7," says Qiang Ren of the Institute of Population Research at Peking University.

Adjusting Birthrates Is Problematic

Zhongwei Zhao, a demographer at the Australian National University in Canberra, agrees. "If you believe the total birthrate is around 2 then there would be no need to relax current family planning policy," he says. "We are worried that [birthrates] may have already fallen to 1.6 or lower. If that is correct, and it continues for 20 or 30 years, then China will have huge problems. The Chinese government needs to consider adjusting the policy now."

Estimates for the ratio of boys to girls, which will also have an impact on future birthrates, are just as variable. The natural human sex ratio is for 103 to 107 boys to be born for every 100 girls. Estimates for China vary from 106 to 123, depending on who is doing the counting.

Ultimately, though, it is already too late to stop the rapid ageing of Chinese society, says Ren, who worked with Lutz on his predictions of future age dependency. But he feels that an increase in birthrates could soften the impact. "In light of our study, we think the Chinese government should consider relaxing its current family planning policies," Ren says.

> ## FAST FACT
>
> China's population policies have resulted in 119 boys being born for every 100 girls. By 2020 there are expected to be 30 million unmarried young Chinese men. Population experts refer to these men as "bare branches" because there will not be enough women for them to mate with.

In the past few years, the government has made some changes. In many regions couples who are both only children can now have a second child, for example. But as China develops further, and urbanisation, better education for women and the higher cost of raising children drive the birthrate still lower, some demographers fear it may be too little too late.

Too Many Men?

The one-child policy and a cultural preference for boys has driven many parents to opt for sex-selective abortion, creating such a huge deficit of girls that by 2025 there could be 30 million fewer women than men aged between 20 and 49, and 47 million fewer by 2050, according to a recent study published in China.

It's a dire situation. Fewer women will further depress national birthrates, placing an additional burden on an already ageing society. There could also be knock-on effects on mental health. "We are concerned about single men being marginalised in poor, rural areas, and the real impacts this will have on their parents, who rely on them, on their communities, and on their psychological well-being," says Li

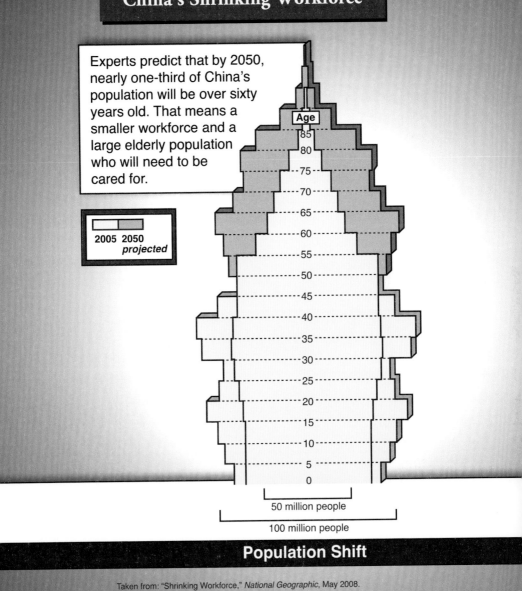

China's Shrinking Workforce

Experts predict that by 2050, nearly one-third of China's population will be over sixty years old. That means a smaller workforce and a large elderly population who will need to be cared for.

2005 2050 projected

Age
85
80
75
70
65
60
55
50
45
40
35
30
25
20
15
10
5
0

50 million people

100 million people

Population Shift

Taken from: "Shrinking Workforce," *National Geographic*, May 2008.

Shuzhuo of the Institute of Population and Development Studies at Xi'an Jiaotong University in Xi'an.

With Chinese society already undergoing dramatic change, it's difficult to predict the more subtle implications of a future society with a glut of males. Some speculate that it will lead to more widespread and open homosexuality. Others fear that an excess of testosterone-driven young men will bring more violence, crime and sexually transmitted disease to the country.

The government would prefer not to find out. In 2003 it launched the "Care for Girls" project, run by the National Population and Family Planning Commission of China. The scheme introduced "pro-girl" policies in 24 counties with the highest excess of boys at birth. Measures included enforcing a ban on sex-selective abortion; improved maternal and child healthcare; financial incentives; and the promotion of gender equality. The result was that the number of boys born for every 100 girls fell from an average of more than 130 to below 120.

[In 2006] the government rolled out the Care for Girls campaign nationwide with the aim of returning the sex ratio at birth to normal within 15 years. In the meantime, China may have to find a way to care for its boys too.

EVALUATING THE AUTHOR'S ARGUMENTS:

Rachel Nowak discusses the birth incentives the Chinese government has used to control the population. Do you think these policies are fair? Why or why not? Based on your answer, what do you think China should do, if anything, to adjust its current population situation? Explain your opinion.

China Is Facing an AIDS Crisis

Xiaoqing Lu and Bates Gill

"Since China's first indigenous case of HIV was identified in 1989, the epidemic has spread numerically and geographically throughout the country."

In the following viewpoint Xiaoqing Lu and Bates Gill argue that China is facing an AIDS crisis. Lu and Gill see a nation at risk: As HIV infections increase among drug users, migrant farm workers, and sex-trade workers, they put the general population in jeopardy. One problem is that China has yet to form a comprehensive AIDS policy. Thus, the monitoring, reporting, and treatment of HIV infections goes unchecked. Lu and Gill claim that entire populations may not even know they have HIV, further spreading the virus. While intravenous drug use was once cited as the main transmission for HIV, Lu and Gill see unsafe sex practices becoming the new major cause. Specifically, Lu and Gill note that socially, China has become more accepting of homosexuality, premarital and extramarital sex, and the sex industries. Furthermore, as exchanges of "risky behaviors" between the general population and China's growing transient population may be on the rise, the entire country may become at risk. Lu and Gill conclude that China must immediately step up its efforts in AIDS education, awareness, and prevention if risk of a full-scale AIDS epidemic is to be thwarted.

Lu is a research associate at the Center for Strategic and International Studies (CSIS) Task Force on HIV/AIDS. Gill is the director of the Stockholm International Peace Research Institute (SIPRI).

AS YOU READ, CONSIDER THE FOLLOWING QUESTIONS:
1. In which five provinces do three-quarters of all HIV-positive Chinese live?
2. According to the authors, what percentage of suspected HIV-positive people are unaware of their infection?
3. According to data collected in 2005, how many of the seventy thousand new cases of AIDS reported were spread through sexual transmission?

China presents one of the largest and most difficult challenges for the worldwide HIV/AIDS epidemic. Since China's first indigenous case of HIV was identified in 1989, the epidemic has spread numerically and geographically throughout the country. Today, HIV-positive people are present in all 31 Chinese provinces, municipalities, and autonomous regions, with about three-quarters of these people living in five Chinese provinces: Yunnan, Henan, Xinjiang, Guangxi, and Guangdong.

Difficulties in Monitoring the HIV Epidemic

The most recent official estimates indicate that as of the end of 2005, there were approximately 650,000 people living with HIV/AIDS in China. Among them, there are an estimated 75,000 people living with AIDS. These figures place the national HIV prevalence at 0.05 percent. In 2005, there were an estimated 70,000 new HIV infections and an estimated 25,000 AIDS deaths.[1] . . .

Although the new estimated figure of approximately 650,000 HIV-positive people is lower than that previously believed, there is no room for complacency. According to Chinese official statistics, there were

1. According to the Joint United Nations Programme on HIV/AIDS, as of 2008 there were an estimated 700,000 people with HIV in China, and about 39,000 deaths in 2007 were AIDS related.

only 191,565 cumulative cases of HIV infection tested and confirmed as of the end of 2006. Experts believe that some half a million or more people in China, or about 80 percent of those believed to be HIV positive, do not know their status, and the government does not know who they are. This is largely due to the lack of a more comprehensive surveillance and testing system that reaches marginalized populations. This gap has obvious implications for the continued spread of HIV in the country.

At-Risk Groups Show Dramatic Increase in HIV

Figures are more troubling among certain at-risk groups. Prevalence among intravenous drug users (IDUs) tripled from 1.95 percent in 1998 to 6.48 percent in 2004—and in some severely affected regions had increased by up to 86.54 percent as of 2005. As of the end of 2005, there are approximately 288,000 drug users living with HIV/AIDS. Ministry of Public Security data suggests that the number of

An HIV-infected patient and her infected daughter receive treatment at a clinic in Anhul province, China. The rising HIV rates are due to increased intravenous drug use and sexual contact.

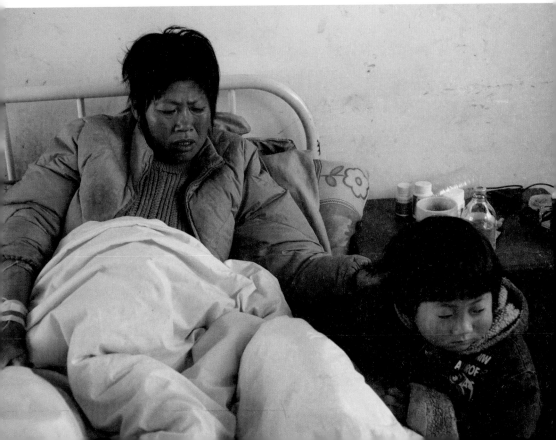

registered drug users has risen steadily at a rate of about 122 percent per year, from 70,000 in 1990 to 1.16 million in 2005. The total number of drug users, including those unregistered, is thought to be much higher, with one estimate placing the figure at 3.5 million.

The most commonly used drug is heroin, which accounts for 85 percent of total reported drug use. Sharing injection equipment is common. Meanwhile, prevalence among commercial sex workers (CSWs) has risen from 0.02 percent in 1996 to 0.93 percent in 2004, a remarkable jump of nearly 50-fold.

FAST FACT

The United Nations Programme on AIDS projects China could have between 10 and 15 million HIV cases by the year 2010—equal to the entire population of Greece.

In addition, several emerging factors—the increase in China's sex trade, increasing premarital and extramarital sex, greater social tolerance for homosexuality and men having sex with men, and risky behavior in the "floating population" of migrant workers—could serve as a bridge to spread the epidemic into the general population. Among pregnant women in high-risk areas, HIV prevalence has grown dramatically, from nil in 1997 to 0.38 percent in 2004. In some provinces, such as Yunnan, Henan, and Xinjiang, HIV-prevalence rates exceed 1 percent among pregnant women and among persons who receive premarital and clinical HIV testing. This meets the criteria of the Joint United Nations Program on HIV/AIDS (UNAIDS) for a "generalized epidemic."

The AIDS Epidemic Threatens the General Public

The source of HIV infection is another indicator of how the disease may be moving toward a more generalized epidemic in China. For example, past estimates suggested that over two-thirds of Chinese HIV cases were contracted through intravenous drug use with infected needles. Data in 2005, however, show that of all persons living with HIV in China today, about 44.3 percent were infected through intravenous drug use, 43.6 percent were infected through sexual contact, 10.7 percent through tainted blood or blood product, and 1.4

percent through mother-to-child transmission. According to a report jointly released by the Chinese Ministry of Health (MOH) and the China Center for Disease Control and Prevention (China CDC), of the 70,000 new HIV infections recorded in 2005, nearly half contracted the virus through sexual contact. Patients infected through sexual transmission are the fastest growing group in China. Unsafe sex has, for the first time, overtaken intravenous drug use as the primary cause of new HIV infections, raising new concerns that the epidemic will spread from high-risk groups to the general public.

While illegal and unsanitary blood collection practices have been significantly reduced in China, the number of persons contracting HIV through unsafe sex will increase in the years ahead due to a rise in commercial sex and extramarital sex. According to Chinese vice minister of health Wang Longde, national surveillance figures indicate that the "epidemic is spreading from high-risk groups to ordinary people, and that China is in a critical period for AIDS prevention." . . .

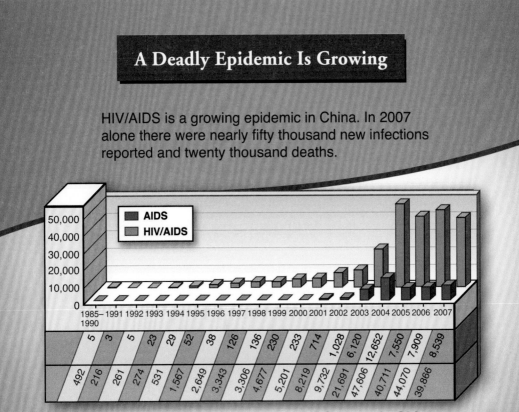

A Deadly Epidemic Is Growing

HIV/AIDS is a growing epidemic in China. In 2007 alone there were nearly fifty thousand new infections reported and twenty thousand deaths.

Legend: AIDS, HIV/AIDS

	1985–1990	1991	1992	1993	1994	1995	1996	1997	1998	1999	2000	2001	2002	2003	2004	2005	2006	2007
AIDS	5	3	5	23	29	52	38	126	136	230	233	714	1,028	6,120	12,652	7,550	7,909	8,539
HIV/AIDS	492	216	261	274	531	1,567	2,649	3,343	3,306	4,677	5,201	8,219	9,732	21,691	47,606	40,711	44,070	39,866

Annual reported HIV positives and AIDS cases in China

Taken from: Joint United Nations Programme on HIV/AIDS (UNAIDS) China, 2008.

AIDS Policies Are Muddled by Bureaucracy

Combating HIV/AIDS is still largely seen as a "health problem" to be tackled by the Ministry of Health, rather than as a broader socio-economic challenge requiring a more comprehensive and coordinated response across the governmental and nongovernmental spectrum. China's government system remains highly "stovepiped," frustrating coordination between departments and across bureaus. Although the central government has called for closer collaboration among various government agencies, and there is increasing interagency collaboration, implementation of effective policy at local levels still remains challenging.

A debilitated public health system, particularly in rural areas where HIV is hitting hardest, undermines an effective response to HIV/AIDS. Overall, resources and capacity are lacking at many levels. Medical professionals lack the expertise and necessary incentives to treat HIV/AIDS patients as well as the necessary equipment and technologies to properly diagnose, counsel, treat, monitor, and care for them. The central government has placed increasing responsibility for financing health care on local authorities. HIV/AIDS, however, is most prevalent in some of the poorest and most remote parts of China, where there is the least financial capacity to address HIV/AIDS prevention and control. With limited financial resources and trained personnel, it is unclear how policies, such as the "four frees and one care," can be effectively implemented at local levels. Due to inconsistent implementation of national policies across the country, the range of services provided by local governments varies from province to province. In addition, as greater resources have begun to flow into China's anti-HIV effort, both from domestic and international sources, there is also an increased need for program management expertise.

Combating AIDS with Education, Awareness, and Prevention

Stigma and discrimination is another formidable obstacle to the successful implementation of many programs on the ground in China. People who are HIV positive or in high-risk groups still experience discrimination from the general public. Therefore, their needs often go unaddressed. Greater emphasis is needed on HIV education, awareness, and prevention. The government remains poorly equipped to deal with those who are most at risk of contracting and spreading HIV/AIDS, particularly highly stigmatized and marginalized populations, including men who have sex with men (MSM) and persons outside of the formal economy engaged in illegal activities, such as intravenous drug users (IDUs) and commercial sex workers (CSWs).

Most civil society organizations, which have often proven to be most effective in providing outreach to hard-to-access, at-risk, marginalized groups, continue to walk a fine line in China, constantly exercising caution and restraint in their activities to avoid political, legal, and financial complications with local and central authorities. While there are clearly bright spots from many pilot projects over the past four years, the status of civil society organizations remains a sensitive issue in the run-up to the 17th Chinese Communist Party Congress in October 2007 and the Beijing Olympics in the summer of 2008. As a result, there is a continued reluctance to allow a greater role for domestic and international civil society organizations in HIV/AIDS prevention and control in China.

In addition, concerns with the safety of China's blood supply, the lack of second-line drugs in China's national treatment program, and the emergence of HIV-drug resistant strains continue to impede a fully effective response to HIV/AIDS in China.

EVALUATING THE AUTHORS' ARGUMENTS:

In the viewpoint you just read, Xiaoqing Lu and Bates Gill suggest that education, awareness, and prevention are the first steps that any effective HIV/AIDS policy must take. What do you think? Which populations should be targeted? What further actions do you think China should take to decrease the spread of AIDS? Explain your answer.

Chapter 2

What Is the Status of Human Rights and Democracy in China?

Human rights in China has been a subject of controversy since the student demonstrations in Tiananmen Square in June 1989 were brutally repressed by the Chinese government.

China Is Becoming More Democratic

"Potential tools for democracy build up subtly, in ways not factored into conventional democracy measurements, for some time until they suddenly become apparent."

Philip I. Levy, interviewed by Evan Sparks

In the following viewpoint Philip I. Levy argues that China has begun to embrace democratic values. China is one of five Communist countries in the world, and as such, has resisted democracy, the author explains. However, as China experiences increased growth and development, it is shifting from a Communist country to a democratic one. In the past, Chinese leaders strictly controlled and monitored China's people, severely limiting their personal rights. In recent times, however, China's government has allowed its people more freedom and liberty. The author explains that more jobs are available than ever, a middle class has started to emerge, and people have been allowed greater access to information. All these factors are strong indicators of a growing democracy in China, the author concludes.

Levy is an economist and researcher studying international trade and development at the American Enterprise Institute for Public Policy Research (AEI), a private,

Evan Sparks, "China: How Economic Integration Might Foster Democratic Development: An Interview with Philip Levy," *American Enterprise Institute Online,* April 17, 2008. Copyright © 2008 American Enterprise Institute. Reproduced by permission.

nonpartisan, not-for-profit research institution. He was interviewed by Evan Sparks, an editorial assistant at AEI.

AS YOU READ, CONSIDER THE FOLLOWING QUESTIONS:
1. By what percent has the Chinese economy grown, as reported by the author? What bearing has this had on democracy in China?
2. According to the author, what three elements have contributed to economic growth and democratic potential in China?
3. In what way does the author think China's hosting of the 2008 summer Olympics indicate it is undergoing a democratic shift?

This summer [August 2008], China will host the summer Olympics for the first time. Its international debut as a super-power is already being hampered by protests in Tibet and Xinjiang, demonstrations along the route of the Olympic torch, and pledges by some Western leaders not to attend the games' opening ceremony. The Chinese leadership's crackdown no doubt chagrined those in democracies who advocated giving China the games. In 2001, the *New York Times* editorialized that even though China's human rights record was poor, "there is reason to hope that the bright spotlight the Olympics can shine on the Chinese government's behavior over the next seven years could prove beneficial to those in China who would like to see their country evolve into a more tolerant and democratic society." Now that the People's Republic is in the spotlight, there is little in the way of visible evolution toward democracy.

Democracy Is Growing in China

But might China be evolving *subtly* toward democracy? That is Philip Levy's intriguing argument in a new AEI [American Enterprise Institute] working paper, "Economic Integration and Incipient Democracy." Whereas conventional democratization theory focuses on benchmarks and indicators of progress on the road to popular rule, Levy suggests that we are overlooking an increased *potential* for change. "The enhanced potential for progress comes from an increase in the means for achieving democratic change," he writes. Levy freely acknowledges that "China's on the absolute bottom" on scales of democratization.

the Yangtze and Yellow rivers, which derive much of their water from glaciers in Tibet, would overflow as the glaciers melted and then dry up. And both Chinese and international scientists now warn that due to rising sea levels, Shanghai could be submerged by 2050.

EVALUATING THE AUTHORS' ARGUMENTS:

In the viewpoint you just read, Elizabeth C. Economy uses many examples and statistics to support her claim that China is on the brink of environmental disaster. In the following viewpoint Yingling Liu paints a different picture of China's environmental status. In a few sentences, explain each author's main reasons for arguing what they do. Then explain how you think they came to such different conclusions about the state of China's environment.

the Chinese government deems about 30 percent of the river water throughout the country to be unfit for use in agriculture or industry. As a result, nearly 700 million people drink water contaminated with animal and human waste. The World Bank has found that the failure to provide fully two-thirds of the rural population with piped water is a leading cause of death among children under the age of five and is responsible for as much as 11 percent of the cases of gastrointestinal cancer in China.

Severe Water Pollution

One of the problems is that although China has plenty of laws and regulations designed to ensure clean water, factory owners and local officials do not enforce them. A 2005 survey of 509 cities revealed that only 23 percent of factories properly treated sewage before disposing of it. According to another report, today one-third of all industrial wastewater in China and two-thirds of household sewage are released untreated. Recent Chinese studies of two of the country's most important sources of water—the Yangtze and Yellow rivers—illustrate the growing challenge. The Yangtze River, which stretches all the way from the Tibetan Plateau to Shanghai, receives 40 percent of the country's sewage, 80 percent of it untreated. In 2007, the Chinese government announced that it was delaying, in part because of pollution, the development of a $60 billion plan to divert the river in order to supply the water-starved cities of Beijing and Tianjin. The Yellow River supplies water to more than 150 million people and 15 percent of China's agricultural land, but two-thirds of its water is considered unsafe to drink and 10 percent of its water is classified as sewage. In early 2007, Chinese officials announced that over one-third of the fish species native to the Yellow River had become extinct due to damming or pollution.

China's leaders are also increasingly concerned about how climate change may exacerbate their domestic environmental situation. In the spring of 2007, Beijing released its first national assessment report on climate change, predicting a 30 percent drop in precipitation in three of China's seven major river regions—around the Huai, Liao, and Hai rivers—and a 37 percent decline in the country's wheat, rice, and corn yields in the second half of the century. It also predicted that

But he points to three changes within China that may indicate the growth of democratic potential—there and elsewhere.

The three elements of democratic potential are also necessary for the dramatic—upwards of 10 percent—economic growth that China has enjoyed. They are communications technology, the rise of alternative leaders, and rule of law. All have sprung up in China along with greater integration into the world economy, and all pose, to some extent, a threat to the Chinese regime. If you were the Chinese leadership, Levy says, "you would not want 400 million cell phones floating around." It's difficult to reverse these trends, leaving the Chinese government in a potentially perilous situation. "They face some difficult choices," Levy adds. "To the extent that they are gaining legitimacy from the economic well-being and the prosperity, a lot of these tools of democracy come with it. They're essentially dual-use technologies." These potential tools for democracy build up subtly, in ways not factored into conventional democracy measurements, for some time until they suddenly become apparent. "In short," says Levy, "they can be seen. We're just not looking."

Which is not to say that incipient democracy happens fast. Levy pointed to the centuries-long incubation of liberal traditions in Great

China's hosting of the Olympic Games in 2008 put pressure on the government to modify its human rights policies.

Britain and its colonies. "If you're measuring year by year," he adds, "you wouldn't expect to see much." In an echo of Zhou Enlai's[1] assessment of the French Revolution as "too soon to tell," it may have been far too presumptuous to have expected visible democratic progress in China in the years before the Olympic Games.

Free Trade Increases Democratic Potential in China

Levy did not work closely on China issues until joining the State Department's policy planning staff in 2005, where he worked on, among other things, the [George W.] Bush administration's "responsible stakeholder" policy toward Beijing. Levy had previously focused on trade issues, first as a senior economist at the President's Council of Economic Advisers and as a professor at Yale. And there is indeed a trade component to Levy's theory. The emergence of these subtle indicators of incipient democracy has been a result of China's growing trade ties with the outside world. "Free trade has been having an effect," he said. "It's very hard to imagine that you'd see things like the Xiamen protests [over pollution], like [the protest over the monorail] through Shanghai . . . in the time of Mao."[2]

> **FAST FACT**
>
> According to the British Broadcasting Company, 86 percent of Chinese say they are happy with the direction in which their country is heading.

The response from the developed world, then, should be to continue trade with China. "You have a substantially greater chance of democracy in China with the kind of economic integration—the trade—that they've had than you would if China had been off in isolation."

Concerns about human rights, security issues, and product safety in China, combined with fears of globalization and the weakening dollar, have clouded the outlook for further free trade. With a potentially disastrous Olympics coming up, will there be any stomach for closer

1. The first premier of the People's Republic of China and a key player in the Communist Party's rise to power.
2. Mao Tse-tung was the Communist leader of the People's Republic of China from 1949 to 1976.

China Is Not Necessarily Becoming More Democratic

James Mann

"We have to stop taking it for granted that China is heading inevitably for political liberalization and democracy."

In the following viewpoint James Mann argues that despite its strong economic growth and emergence in the international marketplace, China is not becoming more democratic. He explains that the Chinese government continues to solidly operate as an autocracy, with the Communist Party maintaining strong control over the country and its people. It does not support democratic ideals, such as the belief that all members of society are equal and that all people should have personal freedom and liberty. In fact, says Mann, three tenets of democracy that China's political system specifically does not support are freedom of political expression, freedom of speech, and freedom of the press. Instead, China routinely censors its media, treats criminals inhumanely, and punishes all opposition. Given this, Mann cautions Americans against assuming that China's booming economy and the fact that its citizens are increasingly enjoy-

James Mann, "America's China Fantasy," *American Prospect,* February 19, 2007. Reproduced with permission from *The American Prospect,* 11 Beacon Street, Suite 1120, Boston, MA 02108.

ing Western products means it is becoming more politically open. Democracy looks especially doomed in China because it is not supported by the middle class, explains Mann. For all these reasons, he concludes that China is far from becoming a democratic nation.

Mann is author-in-residence at Johns Hopkins University's School of Advanced International Studies. He has written extensively about China and is the author of *The China Fantasy: How Our Leaders Explain Away Chinese Repression* and *About Face: A History of America's Curious Relationship with China, from Nixon to Clinton.*

AS YOU READ, CONSIDER THE FOLLOWING QUESTIONS:

1. According to the author, what effect would free elections have on current Chinese leaders?
2. What percent of China's people make up the urban middle class, according to the author?
3. How many people does Mann say belong to China's Communist Party?

America has been operating with the wrong paradigm for China. Day after day, U.S. officials carry out policies based upon premises about China's future that are at best questionable and at worst downright false.

The mistake lies in the very assumption that political change—and with it, eventually, democracy—is coming to China, that China's political system is destined for far-reaching liberalization. Yet the [President George W.] Bush administration hasn't thought much about what it might mean for the United States and the rest of the world to have a repressive one-party state in China three decades from now. For while China will certainly be a richer and more powerful country in 30 years, it could still be an autocracy of one form or another. Its leadership (the Communist Party, or whatever else it calls itself in the future) may not be willing to tolerate organized political opposition any more than it does today.

That is a prospect with profound implications for the United States and the rest of the world. And it is a prospect that our current paradigm of an inevitably changing China cannot seem to envision. . . .

Democracy Is a Threat to China's Leaders

The American people were told many years ago that bringing China into the international economic system would help change the Chinese political system. Now, American workers may well wonder whether this argument was merely a cruel hoax. Nor has the strategy of integration been such a blessing for ordinary Chinese. To be sure, China as a whole is more prosperous than it has ever been, but this new prosperity is enjoyed mostly by the urban middle class, not by the country's overworked, underpaid factory laborers or by the hundreds of millions of peasants in the countryside.

Indeed, it is precisely because the regime knows how restive and disenchanted the Chinese people are that it refuses to open up to any form of democracy. The Chinese leaders know that they could be thrown out of office if there were free and open elections. Democracy, or even an organization calling for future democracy, is a threat to the existing political and economic order in China. That is why the regime continues to repress all forms of organized dissent and political opposition. It is also why China's new class of managers and executives, who profit from keeping wages low, support the regime in its ongoing repression.

China's Middle Class May Not Favor Democracy

A few years ago, the *New York Times* columnist Nicholas D. Kristof gave voice to one of the most common American misconceptions about China's political future. Reflecting on how China had progressed and where it was headed, Kristof wrote, "[Hard-liners] knew that after the Chinese could watch Eddie Murphy, wear tight pink dresses and struggle over what to order at Starbucks, the revolution was finished. No middle class is content with more choices of coffees than of candidates on a ballot."

Once people are eating at McDonald's or wearing clothes from The Gap, American writers rush to proclaim that these people are becoming like us, and that their political system is therefore becoming like ours. But will the newly enriched, Starbucks-sipping, condo-buying, car-driving denizens of China's largest cities in fact become the vanguard for democracy in China? Or is it possible that China's middle-class elite will either fail to embrace calls for a democratic China or turn out to be a driving force in *opposition* to democracy?

Uprisings Threaten Democratic Development

China's emerging urban middle class, after all, is merely a small proportion of the country's overall population—far smaller than its counterparts in Taiwan or South Korea. There are an estimated 800 million to 900 million Chinese peasants—most of them living in rural areas, although 100 million or more are working or trying to find jobs as migrants on the margins of Chinese cities. If China were to have nationwide elections, and if peasants were to vote their own interests, then the urban middle class would lose. The margin would not be close. On an electoral map of China, the biggest cities—Shanghai, Beijing, Tianjin, Guangzhou, and the others—might look something like the small gold stars on the Chinese flag: They would be surrounded by a sea of red. Add together the populations of China's 10 largest cities and you get a total of some 62 million people. That number is larger than the population of France or Britain or Italy. But it is still only about 5 percent of China's overall population of 1.3 billion.

If you are a multinational company trying to sell consumer products, then the rapid rise in spendable income in China's largest cities is of staggering importance. When it comes to any national elections, however, that new Chinese middle class is merely a drop in the bucket. Those in China's urban avant-garde have every reason to fear that they would be outvoted.

China's urban residents have an even greater reason to fear democracy: The Communist Party has not exactly been evenhanded in its treatment of urban residents vis-à-vis peasants. On the contrary: Its policies have strongly favored the cities over the countryside. This is why there has been a wave of protests in the countryside, arising out of land seizures, local taxes, disputes over village elections, and similar controversies. It is also why the Chinese regime has been, in recent years, particularly fearful of mass movements that might sweep through the countryside and undermine the Communist Party's control. Looking

> **FAST FACT**
>
> Reporters Without Borders ranks China 163 out of 169 countries for freedom of the press, calling it the world's "largest prison for journalists." Freedom of the press is regarded as an important cornerstone of democracy.

Pro-democracy protesters demonstrate in Hong Kong against China's human rights record. The Chinese government continues to crack down on pro-democracy advocates in China.

at Falun Gong, the quasi-religious movement that began to take hold during the 1990s, the Chinese leadership was haunted by a specter from the past: the Taiping Rebellion, which swept out of middle China in the 19th century and shook the Qing Dynasty to its foundations.

The Communist Party Wields the Most Power

What lies behind the Chinese Communist Party's monopoly on power and its continuing repression of dissent? The answer usually offered is the Communist Party itself—that the party and its more than 70 million members are clinging to their own power and privileges. This is certainly part of the answer, but not all of it. As China's economy has thrived in recent years, strong economic and social forces have also emerged in Chinese society that will seek to protect the existing order and their own economic interests. The new middle class in Chinese cities is coming to favor the status quo nearly as much as does the Communist Party itself.

Data from the International Monetary Fund shows that nondemocratic countries on average have more robust economies than democratic ones. Experts use this to argue that China's economic growth does not necessarily mean it will become a democracy.

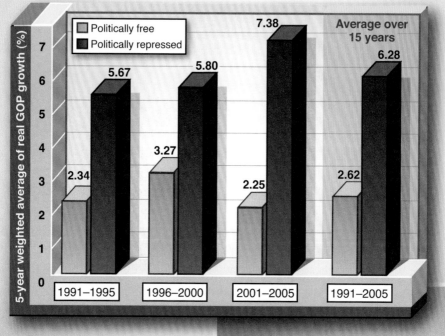

Taken from: Kevin Hassett, "Does Economic Success Require Democracy?" *American*, May/June 2007.

Why do we assume that what follows the Chinese Communist Party's eventual fall will necessarily be political liberalization or democracy? One can envision other possibilities. Suppose, for example, that the party proves over the next decade to be no better at combating the country's endemic corruption than it has been over the past decade. Public revulsion over this corruption reaches the point where the Chinese people take to the streets; leaders find they cannot depend on troops to quell these demonstrations; the Communist Party finally gives way. Even then, would the result be Chinese democracy? Not necessarily. China's urban middle class might choose to align itself with the military and the security apparatus to support some other form of authoritarian regime, arguing that it is necessary to do so in order to keep the economy running.

Democracy Is Not Necessarily a Reality

The underlying premise of the U.S. integration strategy is that we can put off the question of Chinese democracy. But two or three decades from now, it may be too late. By then, China will be wealthier, and the entrenched interests opposing democracy will probably be much stronger. By then, China will be so thoroughly integrated into the world financial and diplomatic systems that, because of the country's sheer commercial power, there will be no international support for any movement to open up China's political system.

What should the United States do to encourage democratic change in China? A detailed list of policies can emerge only after we first rid ourselves of the delusions and the false assumptions upon which our China policy has long been based.

Above all, we have to stop taking it for granted that China is heading inevitably for political liberalization and democracy. President [George W.] Bush has continued to repeat the American mantra about China, every bit as much as did his predecessors. "As China reforms its economy, its leaders are finding that once the door to freedom is opened even a crack, it cannot be closed," Bush declared in one typical speech. Such words convey a heartwarming sense of hopefulness about China, but they do not match the reality of China itself, where doors are regularly opened by more than a crack and then closed again.

EVALUATING THE AUTHOR'S ARGUMENTS:

In this viewpoint James Mann argues that access to consumer products such as McDonald's, Starbucks, and clothes from the Gap will not cause people to demand more political freedom. What do you think? Can exposing people to a wider range of product choices make them demand more political choices? Or are the two unrelated?

Viewpoint
3

Censorship Is a Serious Problem in China

Paul Wiseman

"The Chinese government . . . is arguably the world's best at controlling what its people see."

In the following viewpoint Paul Wiseman argues that censorship is a common and serious problem in China. China restricts its people's access to information by tightly controlling what information they see, hear, and read. Wiseman explains that any information or material that criticizes the government's policies, including news stories, blogs, television, and movies, is either gravely distorted or suppressed altogether. In some cases Chinese citizens are not told the truth about important events; in other cases the government shares only information that makes the administration or the Communist Party look good. As a result the Chinese people are misinformed about current events and history, which keeps them powerless. Wiseman concludes that the suppression of information undermines the Chinese people's basic human right to freedom of information and independence of thought.

Paul Wiseman, "Cracking the 'Great Firewall' of China's Web Censorship," *USA Today,* April 23, 2008. Copyright © 2008 USA TODAY, a division of Gannett Co. Inc. Reproduced by permission.

Wiseman is a regular contributor to *USA Today,* and he covers international news in Asia and the Middle East.

AS YOU READ, CONSIDER THE FOLLOWING QUESTIONS:
1. What are "hacktivists"? What role do they play in the fight against censorship in China?
2. What two events does the author say caused Chinese officials to step up Web censorship in March 2008?
3. Explain the main difference in the way the United States and China channel their Internet traffic.

I f an Internet user in China searches for the word "persecution," he or she is likely to come up with a link to a blank screen that says "page cannot be displayed."

The same is true of searches for "Tibetan independence," "democracy movements" or stranger sounding terms such as "oriental red space time"—code for an anti-censorship video made secretly by reporters at China's state TV station.

It's a reflection of the stifling, bizarre and sometimes dangerous world of Internet censorship in China. The communist government in Beijing is intensifying its efforts to control what its citizens can read and discuss online as political tensions rise ahead of this summer's [2008] Olympic Games.

China Is the World's Best Censor

Fighting the censors every step of the way is an army of self-described "hacktivists" such as Bill Xia, a Chinese-born software engineer who lives in North Carolina. Xia and others are engaged in a kind of technological arms race, inventing software and using other tactics to allow ordinary Chinese to beat the "Great Firewall of China" and access information on sensitive subjects such as Chinese human rights and Tibet, the province where pro-independence sentiment has boiled over in recent months.

Invoking the hit science-fiction movie *The Matrix,* Xia has compared what he does to giving Chinese Web surfers a "red pill" that lets them see reality for the first time. He spends long nights struggling to outfox an opponent—the Chinese government—that is arguably the world's best at controlling what its people see.

"They are very smart," Xia says. "We have to move very quickly."

To Americans and other Westerners, it might seem odd that Internet censorship is still possible at a time when YouTube, satellite TV and online chat rooms produce an overwhelming flow of real-time news and data. Yet authoritarian regimes from Cuba to Saudi Arabia to Pakistan rely on a mix of sophisticated technology and old-fashioned intimidation to ensure that dissent can be repressed, even in the Information Age.

No one does it quite like China, which has proved that old-school communist apparatchiks [members of the party] could tame something as wild as the Web. China has the world's "most sophisticated" Internet filtering system, according to the OpenNet Initiative, an academic cooperative that tracks censorship issues.

China's Government Uses Censorship to Suppress Opposition

At the heart of China's censorship efforts is a delicate balancing act.

Unlike communist North Korea, which bans online access to its general population, China is encouraging Internet usage as it rushes to construct a modern economy. [In 2008], the number of Internet users in China surpassed the USA for the first time, hitting 233 million by the end of March. However, China's government does not tolerate opposition and is wary of the variety of views and information the Web brings.

[The March 2008] pro-independence riots in Tibet, and the accompanying furor that followed the international relay of the Olympic torch, have led Chinese officials to step up their Web censorship. News articles and video clips concerning Tibet were banned for several days. Xia expects the censorship will tighten further in the coming months because "many human rights organizations will be trying to get their voices heard" during the Olympic Games.

"There will be lots of news out there," says Xia, who admits he had little interest in politics until the Chinese government banned the spiritual group Falun Gong in 1999 and started persecuting its members. Xia is a member of the group.

"Lots of unexpected things are going to happen," he says.

Chinese youths surf the Web at a Beijing Internet café. The Chinese government controls all access to and censors the Internet in China.

China Restricts Web Access

The most basic tool at the Chinese government's disposal—and, perhaps, the one most easily circumvented by dissidents—is to ban access within China to websites such as Voice of America or to certain stories that contain sensitive words and phrases. For example, several recent USA TODAY stories about Tibet are currently blocked within China.

The Great Firewall of China

China is among just a handful of nations that practice pervasive censoring of political material on the Internet.

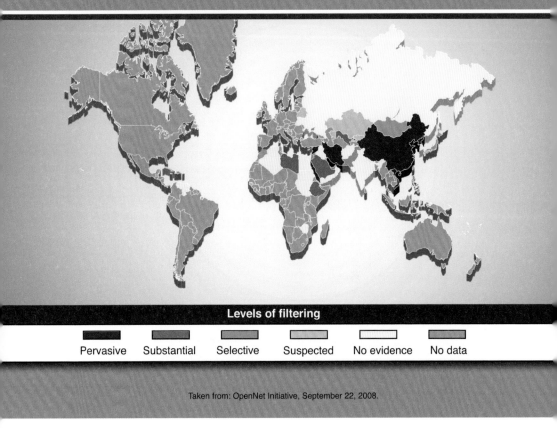

Levels of filtering

Pervasive   Substantial   Selective   Suspected   No evidence   No data

Taken from: OpenNet Initiative, September 22, 2008.

Other censorship methods are more blunt. [In April 2008] Hu Jia, an activist on AIDS and other issues, was sentenced to 3½ years in jail for articles he wrote for Boxun.com, a U.S.-based Chinese-language website that is banned in China. At least 48 cyberdissidents are behind bars in China, according to Reporters Without Borders.

Chinese officials with the Ministry of Information Industry, the State Council Information Office and other agencies declined to comment on why China restricts content on the Internet.

Past explanations by the government focus on the need to prevent "harmful" content such as pornography and terrorism from reaching citizens.

Even those "hacktivists" who live outside the country apparently face risks. Peter Li—a Chinese-born, Princeton-educated computer specialist—says he learned that two years ago when he answered the doorbell at his home in suburban Atlanta.

Three men burst inside, beat him, bound him and gagged him with duct tape, he says. Speaking Korean and Chinese, they ransacked his filing cabinets and hauled off his two computers. They ignored a TV, a camcorder and other valuables.

The FBI and the local Fulton County, Ga., police still have not found the men responsible for the attack. But Li, who like Xia is a practicing member of Falun Gong, says it was an attempt by the Chinese government to shut him up.

"I know it wasn't a simple robbery," he says.

The Chinese government has denied any involvement in the raid on Li's home.

Censorship Is Widespread

There are a range of other methods China has used to suppress information. Among them:

- *Creating bottlenecks.* In *The Atlantic* magazine [in March 2008], journalist James Fallows noted that Internet traffic to China is channeled through three computer centers—near Beijing, Shanghai and the southern city of Guangzhou.

  In the USA, by contrast, the Internet is designed to avoid traffic jams by allowing information to flow from as many sources as possible. By building in chokepoints, Fallows wrote, "Chinese authorities can easily do something that would be harder in most developed countries: physically monitor all traffic into or out of the country."

- *Checking Internet traffic for subversive material.* This is done in much the same way police dogs sniff airport luggage for illegal drugs. The Chinese install "packet sniffers" and special routers to inspect data as they cruise past the chokepoints. If the detectors spot a Chinese Internet user trying to visit a suspect website—say, one run by Falun Gong—they can block the connection.

A frustrated user might get a message saying: "Site not found." Similarly, Web users can be stopped from leaving subversive comments in online forums. Sometimes they get notes back warning them to behave or apologizing for technical problems.

- *Demanding self-censorship.* Chinese authorities hold commercial websites responsible for what appears on them. In Beijing—where Internet controls are strictest—authorities issue orders to website managers through cellphone text messages and demand that they comply within 30 minutes, according to a report last fall [2007] by Reporters Without Borders.

  When the Internet portal Sina altered the headline of a state media report on the economy, the government accused it of "inciting violence" and excluded it from interviews with important officials for a month. The website NetEase fired two editors after they published a 2006 poll showing that 64% of 10,000 participants would not want to be reborn as Chinese.

- *Issuing propaganda.* Authorities in the southern boomtown of Shenzhen created two cute cartoon cybercops—the male Jingjing and the female Chacha—that pop up on websites to remind Internet users they're being watched. The *Beijing Youth Daily* newspaper quoted a security official admitting that the big-eyed cartoon duo were designed "to intimidate."

  Chinese officials also order websites to reprint official propaganda such as a report encouraging Internet users to abide by online etiquette. . . .

American Companies Let China Censor

China has policed the Internet with assistance from U.S. firms. Cisco Systems, for instance, supplied the original routers China used to monitor Internet traffic. (Cisco has said it didn't tailor its equipment for the Chinese market.)

Google created a censored search engine for China. Outside China, users who search Google Images for "Tiananmen Square" get pictures from the 1989 pro-democracy protests that ended in a crackdown that left hundreds dead—and included the iconic photograph of a lone man staring down a line of Chinese tanks. Inside China, users get only tourist images of Tiananmen Square and the Forbidden City across the street.

Yahoo turned over e-mail that authorities used to jail a Chinese journalist who leaked information about China's attempts to censor coverage of the anniversary of the Tiananmen crackdown. (The companies say they had to comply with Chinese law.)

Despite China's strategies, sophisticated Internet users in the country "can pretty much get as much information as (they) want," says Jeremy Goldkorn, the Beijing-based editor of the China media website danwei.org. "But what (the government does) is make it difficult, so the ordinary person is not going to bother."

EVALUATING THE AUTHOR'S ARGUMENTS:

In this viewpoint Paul Wiseman discusses the role American companies have played in China's censorship of the Internet. What is this role? Do you approve or disapprove of these companies' decisions? Explain your position.

China Is Loosening Its Grip on the Media

Ellen Lee

"Much more information is available in China than ever."

In the following viewpoint Ellen Lee argues that China has relaxed its control over the media. In the past, China had strict policies regarding what information could be shared with Chinese citizens. Every type of media—television, radio, and written news sources—was censored to curb opposition to the government. But the advent of the Internet has brought greater freedom of expression to China's people, explains Lee. Internet users are able to find information on topics that were previously banned and express personal views and political opinions using the Internet's blogs, forums, and social networking tools. The author concludes that the Internet has forced China to relax its grip on the media, and as a result Chinese people are enjoying greater freedom of expression and access to information.

Lee is a technology reporter for the *San Francisco Chronicle.* She has traveled to China on a World Affairs Journalism Fellowship awarded by the International Center for

Journalists and sponsored by the Ethics and Excellence in Journalism Foundation.

AS YOU READ, CONSIDER THE FOLLOWING QUESTIONS:
1. What is the "Great Firewall of China," as described by Lee?
2. Who is Guo Liang, and what about the digital age does he say makes it difficult for the Chinese government to censor information?
3. According to the author, what percent of Internet users believe the Web should be somewhat censored so that pornography and violence do not become ubiquitous?

Just days after David Wang produced a mock newscast criticizing Taiwanese officials and uploaded the clip to Tudou, a popular video sharing site in China, it disappeared. What's surprising is not that it was censored—but that it remained online as long as it did.

His experience illustrates how the Internet is challenging China's status quo.

Technology Gives Media More Freedom

Blogs, forums, social networking, video sharing and other community-oriented sites—known as Web 2.0—depend on users expressing their opinions. Meanwhile, peer-to-peer services make it easier to share information, from a bootleg copy of the latest Hollywood film to a documentary about Tiananmen Square.

The result is the chipping away of what's referred to as the Great Firewall of China, by which the government tries to control online content even as the country is lured to nurture Internet development for economic reasons.

"You could not see such things happen before in China because of the controlled media," said Isaac Mao, an Internet entrepreneur in Shanghai. Now, he said, "You can see grassroots-based technology helping people become empowered."

The Internet Allows People to Share Information Easily

For instance, bloggers and citizen journalists armed with cell phones and Internet access have posted photos and videos about everything

Chinese political bloggers watch a session of China's legislature. Blogs, forums, social networking, and video sharing are slowly eroding the Great Firewall of China and the government's ability to censor all the time.

from a neighborhood traffic accident to the recent Sichuan earthquake. In some cases, they challenge government and corporate actions.

Guo Liang, an associate professor at the Chinese Academy of Social Sciences, uses this analogy to describe the Sisyphean [futile] attempts to block the flood of information on the Internet:

"If something happened in the world and there are 10 sources of information on this event, even if I block nine, you can get one. That's enough for you. You don't need the other nine resources. . . . Once you get that information, you can forward that to others.

"This is the digital age," he said. "I don't think it will work to block or filter something."

Accessing New Information Online

One 27-year-old information technology employee from Shanghai, who asked that his name not be used for fear of retaliation, said that through the Internet, he discovered different versions of what happened during China's Cultural Revolution and World War II. A friend shared a documentary about the 1989 Tiananmen Square protest that had been downloaded from an overseas file-sharing service.

"It was completely different from what I learned in school," he said. "It's hard to believe the first time you see a different edition of history. At first I felt it's unbelievable. Then I felt angry because I was deceived for such a long time."

Indeed, tech-savvy Internet users have learned how to circumvent the Chinese government's attempts to shield certain information. In online forums, they substitute certain words, such as using a character that sounds like the actual word. They use peer-to-peer services to download otherwise inaccessible information. And they use tools such as Tor, which lets them surf the Internet anonymously and visit blocked Web sites.

Hong Bu, better known as Keso, a popular pony-tailed blogger in his 40s in Beijing, has openly criticized the Chinese government for blocking sites and censoring content.

"It is not like I want to knock down the government or rise in rebellion against government officials," he said. "It is just a shame that there are many good tools and information that we cannot access and use."

> # FAST FACT
>
> In 2008 the number of Chinese Internet users surpassed American ones. There are more than 253 million Internet users in China, compared with 220 million in the United States.

Pornography and Violence Are Valid Subjects of Censorship

But not all Chinese users believe that the Internet should be completely open. Some entrepreneurs and consumers challenged what they described as the foreign media's biased and overly zealous interest in the country's censorship policies. Much more information is available in China than ever, they said.

A recent survey by the Chinese Academy of Social Sciences found that more than 80 percent of Chinese Internet users said they believe the Internet needs to be managed, with 85 percent believing the government should be responsible and 79 percent saying the Internet companies should be in control. Increasingly, the study also found, Chinese Internet users—41 percent—believe that politics should be controlled online.

China Leads the World in Internet Users

In 2008 the number of Chinese Internet users had grown so much that it surpassed the United States as the nation with the most people online. While the percentage of American Internet users is much greater than China's (71 percent of the American population is online, vs. 17 percent of China's), China's growing Internet use illustrates the extent the Web is affecting the flow of information there.

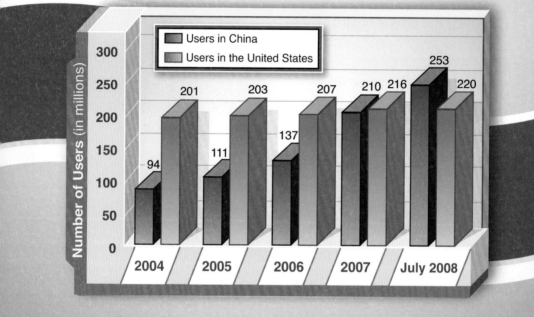

Taken from: Compiled from reports in *USA Today*, Nielson-Net Ratings, *Business Wire*, *Forbes*, and the China Internet Network Information Center (CNNIC).

Guo, the author, said in reviewing their responses that people are worried not so much about political control as they are about maintaining social stability among China's 1.3 billion people and curbing social ills such as pornography and violence.

The Internet Empowers the Chinese People

Xiao Qiang, director of the China Internet Project and an adjunct professor at UC [University of California] Berkeley's journalism school, said that despite the continuing game between the government and

China's Internet users, the shift toward more user participation and self-expression benefits Chinese society, particularly as it becomes part of the daily fabric of life for China's young Internet users.

"It empowers people," he said. "It changes the configuration of the social structure and fabric. We've only seen the beginning."

EVALUATING THE AUTHORS' ARGUMENTS:

In this viewpoint Ellen Lee argues that China is becoming a less-censored place. Paul Wiseman, the author of the previous viewpoint, argues the opposite. After reading both viewpoints, with which author do you agree? What pieces of evidence swayed you? Include them in your answer.

Chapter 3

Does China Pose an International Threat?

A Chinese naval vessel in Tokyo Harbor in 2007 is evidence of China's growing military power.

China Is Poised to Become the Next Superpower

Doug J. Bandow

"China has begun to challenge the US in small ways."

China is poised to become the next world superpower, argues Doug J. Bandow in the following viewpoint. Bandow explains that China has experienced rapid economic growth as a result of increased international trading. As such, China has become a more prosperous and powerful nation. This money and power has helped China strengthen its military and build more nuclear weapons. Bandow warns that these changes could allow China to become a new superpower, capable of influencing and dominating other nations. The author predicts that China's development will continue to challenge American dominance in the twenty-first century.

Bandow is a columnist for Antiwar.com, a nonprofit foundation that publishes news and opinion pieces related to wars throughout the world. He is also the author of sev-

Doug J. Bandow, "China Rising: The Next Global Superpower," Antiwar.com, January 26, 2007. Reproduced by permission of the author.

eral books, including *Politics of Plunder* and *Foreign Follies: America's New Global Empire*.

AS YOU READ, CONSIDER THE FOLLOWING QUESTIONS:
1. What three factors does the author say have pushed China to the first rank of nations?
2. By what percent did China's military increase in 2006, according to the author?
3. When do experts predict China will achieve as much regional influence as the United States has?

[In January 2007] China took a small but critical step to end American global dominance. Until now the US and Russia were the only two nations thought capable of making military use of space. But Beijing [China's capital city and political center] dramatically crashed this select club by using a ground-based ballistic missile to destroy an old weather satellite. Although America will remain the globe's military number one for decades, it must begin to contemplate a world in which it no longer stands alone.

China Has Become a First-Rank Nation

China once was the dominant power in Asia, an advanced civilization to which surrounding states paid obeisance. Then internal decay weakened the Chinese empire, which was battered by European colonial powers and a modernizing Japan. In 1949 Communist revolutionaries created a new state, the People's Republic of China (PRC), which suffered through famine, hardship, and repression. Two decades ago, however, the PRC embarked on a reform course.

Rapid economic growth, global trading ties, and expanding diplomatic cooperation have pushed China to the first rank of nations. There are other potential contenders for future international influence—Brazil and India, for instance—but Beijing is likely the next peer competitor to the US. No one knows when, but some day the PRC and America are likely to meet as equals.

China Is Modernizing Its Military

What happens then obviously depends on China's capabilities and intentions. Beijing has emphasized its commitment to peace and prosperity, and it has a substantial interest in both. However, that has not stopped it from developing a military better reflecting its economic potential, "lethal, high-tech capabilities," in the words of Lin Chong-Pin, a Taiwanese analyst.

The anti-satellite test was not the first jolt felt in Washington. Last October [2006] China used a ground-based laser to "blind" an American spy satellite. Although that strike did not impair US capabilities, it presumably was not intended to do so—at this time.

In December 2006 Chinese president Hu Jintao called for the construction of a strong navy. Western analysts fear that China is emerging as a superpower capable of influencing and dominating other countries.

The PRC continues to modernize its nuclear force. Beijing has tested long-range submarine-launched missiles, capable of hitting the continental US from China's littoral waters. Although Beijing remains far behind Washington in the nuclear race, [in the fall of 2006] the Chinese media quoted a military officer stating that the PRC had "already completely ensured that it has second-strike capability," in part because of its ability to destroy American satellites.

In late December [2006] President Hu Jintao called for construction of a strong Chinese navy, one with "blue-water" capabilities [meaning it could compete in open seas]. He told a Communist Party meeting that "We should strive to build a powerful navy that adapts to the needs of our military's historical mission in this new century and at this new stage." Ni Lexiong at the Shanghai Institute of Political Science and Law contends: "Though this does not mean immediate budget increases, it is a strong signal that lays out our future direction." Indeed, China has been acquiring Russian weaponry, including submarines and anti-ship missiles.

Also in December [2006] Beijing issued a military white paper, affirming the PRC's defensive intent while announcing planned enhancements of early-warning systems, anti-missile defenses, and air-strike capabilities. The International Institute for Strategic Studies (IISS) figures that PRC military outlays have trebled over the last decade, and there is no sign that China intends to slow down. Military outlays continue to increase at double digit rates, by 15 percent [in 2006], according to China's official (and significantly understated) figures. Observes Allan Behm, formerly with Australia's Ministry of Defense: "China is becoming more assertive in just about every military field."

China's Military Growth Threatens America

Washington policymakers are getting nervous as a result. A number of hawkish analysts believe Beijing will be America's next enemy. Even

The Effect of China's Rise

While some around the world expect China's economy to reach the size and influence of the United States', opinions are mixed about the resulting implications.

- ■ Mostly positive ■ Equally positive and negative ■ Mostly negative

"If China's economy were to grow to be as large as the U.S. economy, do you think that would be mostly positive, mostly negative, or equally positive and negative?"

Country	Mostly positive	Equally positive and negative	Mostly negative
Mexico	38	16	33
Argentina	34	29	14
United States	9	54	33
Armenia	31	37	12
Ukraine	30	27	12
Poland	22	34	21
Russia	22	34	24
France	20	46	29
Iran	60	15	12
Israel	27	41	17
Thailand	34	25	10
India	28	20	31
Philippines	26	42	17

Taken from: The Chicago Council on Global Affairs, May 25, 2007.

the [George W.] Bush administration has been issuing warnings about China.

For instance, [in 2005] the Defense Department pointed with some concern at the PRC's desire to project power beyond its own region. [In 2006] the Pentagon declared: "Of the major emerging powers, China has the greatest potential to compete militarily with the United States and field disruptive military technologies that over time offset traditional US military advantages absent US counter strategies."

The *Financial Times* reports: "In recent years, the Pentagon has become increasingly alarmed as Beijing has allocated far more on weapons than US military experts had expected. Washington is particularly concerned about the rapid growth in the size of the Chinese navy and also the increased spending on its nuclear forces." Last November [2006] the US-China Economic and Security Review Commission charged: "China is pursuing measures to try to control the seas in the Western Pacific and developing space warfare weapons that would impede US command and control."

The Chinese anti-satellite test reinforces these attitudes. National Security Council spokesman Gordon Johndroe sniffed: "The United States believes China's development and testing of such weapons is inconsistent with the spirit of cooperation that both countries aspire to in the civil space area." Indeed, Jonathan Pollack at the Naval War College worries that "many people in Washington will find that this validates the view of a China threat." . . .

China's Future Challenge Is Apparent

Analysts predict that the PRC will reach regional parity with the US by early mid-century. Observes Chung Min Lee of National University of Singapore: "The People's Liberation Army's (PLA) emphasis on key force modernizations, including more robust submarine forces, a new generation of fighter aircraft and an array of asymmetrical capabilities, means that over the next two to three decades it will come close to becoming a so-called 'theater peer' of the United States." This worries some American analysts. Harvard University's Robert Ross writes: "For the rise of China to pose a direct threat to US security, China must possess sufficient military capabilities to challenge the United States in the western Pacific, including sufficient capability to risk war."

The Rise of China's Economy

Majorities around the world believe that China will soon catch up with the United States economically, preparing it for superpower status.

- China's economy will grow as large
- United States will be larger
- Unsure

"Do you think that it is more likely that someday China's economy will grow to be as large as the U.S. economy or that the U.S. economy will always stay larger than China's?"

Country	China's economy will grow as large	United States will be larger	Unsure
Peru	76	7	17
Argentina	61	24	15
United States	60	5	35
France	69	5	26
Russia	62	18	20
Armenia	47	23	30
Ukraine	43	37	20
Poland	43	31	26
Israel	75	11	14
Iran	64	15	21
South Korea	61	2	37
China	50	12	38
Thailand	39	45	16
Philippines	38	20	42
India	22	42	36

Taken from: The Chicago Council on Global Affairs, May 25, 2007.

China has begun to challenge the US in small ways. After a Chinese submarine stalked an American carrier group last October [2006], Richard Fisher, with the International Assessment and Strategy Center, argued: "This is a harbinger of a stronger Chinese reaction to America's military presence in East Asia." Still, an eventual superpower China might be, but today it can only stalk, not match, US naval power. It will be decades before China is able to deploy sufficient forces along its own shores to counter the units America can employ far distant from its homeland. . . .

Much Depends on China's Relationship with the United States

Irrespective of what America desires, a more powerful PRC seems inevitable. Notes Allan Behm: Beijing "is not going to concede that the US can be the hegemon in space forever." Or anywhere else. Indeed, Kenneth Lieberthal of the University of Michigan argues that "The Chinese wouldn't put it this way themselves. But in their hearts I think they believe that the 21st century is China's century."

Maybe. The 21st century is more likely to be peaceful and prosperous, however, if America and China cooperate to make the 21st century their joint century. There is little harm which the two could not cause if they come to blows. There is little good which the two could not achieve by working together. Much depends—for them, Asia, and the world—upon the future relationship between the US and China.

EVALUATING THE AUTHORS' ARGUMENTS:

In this viewpoint Doug J. Bandow argues that China has all the makings to become the next world superpower—economic wealth, a large population, and military strength. How do you think the author of the following viewpoint, John Pomfret, might respond to this argument? Explain your answer using evidence from both texts.

China Is Not Poised to Become the Next Superpower

John Pomfret

"China is more likely to remain the muscle-bound adolescent of the international system than to become the master of the world."

John Pomfret argues in the following viewpoint that China is not poised to become the next world superpower. Although China has experienced tremendous economic growth and military expansion, Pomfret argues these developments are not significant enough to usurp the United States as a nation of might and influence. He explains that China has too many problems to become a true superpower. These include an elderly workforce, an overrated economy, a potential environmental crisis, and a political ideology that is not attractive to much of the world. As a result, Pomfret says China lacks the internal strength and global influence required to be a superpower. The author urges Americans to stop building up China—it is not likely to overtake the United States in any area as long as these problems remain.

John Pomfret, "China Still Has Long March to Achieve Greatness: It's Big—but So Are Its Problems," *The Washington Post*, August 3, 2008. Reprinted with permission.

Pomfret is a former Beijing bureau chief for the *Washington Post*. He is also the author of *Chinese Lessons: Five Classmates and the Story of the New China*.

AS YOU READ, CONSIDER THE FOLLOWING QUESTIONS:
1. According to Pomfret, what phenomena do some alarmists cite to support China's readiness for twenty-first-century dominance?
2. What about China's demographics hurt its chances of becoming a superpower, according to Pomfret?
3. According to the author, what environmental problem is China likely to face in the year 2030 that will affect its economic growth?

Nikita Khrushchev [premier of the Soviet Union from 1958 to 1964] said the Soviet Union would bury us, but these days, everybody seems to think that China is the one wielding the shovel.

The People's Republic is on the march—economically, militarily, even ideologically. Economists expect its gross domestic product to surpass America's by 2025. Its submarine fleet is reportedly growing five times faster than Washington's. Even its capitalist authoritarianism is called a real alternative to the West's liberal democracy. China, the drumbeat goes, is ready to dominate the 21st century the way the United States dominated the 20th.

Except that it's not.

China Is Not Ready to Be a Superpower

Ever since I returned to the United States in 2004 from my last posting to China, I've been struck by the breathless way we talk about that country. So often perceptions of the place have more to do with how we look at ourselves than with what's actually happening over there.

Worried about the U.S. education system? China's becomes a model. Fretting about military readiness? China's missiles pose a threat. Concerned about slipping U.S. global influence? China seems ready to take our place.

But will China really be another superpower? I doubt it.

I'm not a China basher. I first went to China in 1980 as a student, and I've followed its remarkable transformation over the past 28 years. I met my wife there and call it a second home. I'm hardly expecting China to implode. But its dream of dominating the century won't be a reality any time soon.

Too many constraints are built into the country's social, economic and political systems. For four big reasons—dire demographics, an overrated economy, an environment under siege and an ideology that doesn't travel well—China is more likely to remain the muscle-bound adolescent of the international system than to become the master of the world.

Chinese citizens line up to get water in Chenzou City, China. Water shortages are just one of the many problems impeding China's rise as a superpower.

A Rising Elderly Population Will Hurt the Economy

In the West, China is known as "the factory to the world," the land of unlimited labor where millions are eager to leave the hardscrabble countryside for a chance to tighten screws in microwaves. If the country is going to rise to superpowerdom, says conventional wisdom, it will do so on the back of its work force.

But China's demographics stink. No country is aging faster than the People's Republic, which is on track to become the first nation in the world to get old before it gets rich. Because of the Communist Party's notorious one-child-per-family policy, the average number of children born to a Chinese woman has dropped from 5.8 in the 1970s to 1.8 today—below the rate of 2.1 that would keep the population stable. Meanwhile, life expectancy has shot up, from just 35 in 1949 to more than 73 today. Economists worry that as the working-age population shrinks, labor costs will rise, significantly eroding one of China's key competitive advantages.

Worse, Chinese demographers such as Li Jianmin of Nankai University now predict a crisis with China's elderly, a group that will balloon from 100 million people older than 60 today to 334 million by 2050, including a staggering 100 million age 80 or older. How will China care for them? With pensions? Fewer than 30 percent of urban dwellers have them, and none of the 700 million farmers do.

And China's state-funded pension system makes Social Security look like Fort Knox. Nicholas Eberstadt, a demographer and economist at the American Enterprise Institute, calls China's demographic time bomb "a slow-motion humanitarian tragedy in the making."

China's Economy Is Overrated

Not a month goes by without some Washington think tank crowing that China's economy is overtaking America's. But there are two problems with their predictions. First, in the universe where these

© 2008 Vince O'Farrell, *The Illawarra Mercury* (Australia), and PoliticalCartoons.com.

reports are generated, China's graphs always go up, never down. Second, while the documents may include some nuance, it vanishes when the studies are reported to the rest of us.

One important nuance we keep forgetting is the sheer size of China's population: about 1.3 billion, more than four times that of the United States. China should have a big economy.

But on a per capita basis, the country isn't a dragon. It's a medium-size lizard, sitting in 109th place on the International Monetary Fund's World Economic Outlook Database, between Swaziland and Morocco. China's economy is large, but its average living standard is low and will remain so for a very long time.

The big number wheeled out to prove that China is eating our economic lunch is the U.S. trade deficit with China, which last year [2007] hit $256 billion. But nearly 60 percent of China's exports are churned out by companies not owned by Chinese. When it comes to high-tech exports such as computers and electronic goods, 89 percent come from non-Chinese-owned companies. China is part of the global system, but it's still the low-cost assembly and manufacturing part—and foreign firms are reaping the lion's share of the profits.

On the Brink of Environmental Crisis
In 2004, when my family and I moved to Los Angeles, the smog capital of the United States, my son's frequent asthma attacks and chronic chest infections stopped. When people asked why we'd moved to L.A., I started joking, "For the air."

China's environmental woes are no joke. [In 2008], China will surpass the United States as the world's No. 1 emitter of greenhouse gases. China is the largest depleter of the ozone layer and the largest polluter of the Pacific Ocean. Sixteen of the world's 20 most polluted cities are in China; 70 percent of its lakes and rivers are polluted and half its population lacks clean drinking water.

By 2030, the nation will face a water shortage equal to the amount it consumes today. Factories in the northwest have already been forced out of business because there just isn't any water. Even Chinese government economists estimate environmental troubles shave 10 percent off the country's gross domestic product annually.

China's Ideology Is Not Exportable
Then there's *Kung Fu Panda*, which embodies the final reason why China won't be a superpower. The recent Hollywood smash, about a panda who uses ancient Chinese teachings to turn himself into a kung fu warrior, broke Chinese box-office records and caused handwringing among the country's glitterati.

"The film's protagonist is China's national treasure, and all the elements are Chinese, but why didn't we make such a film?" Wu Jiang, president of the China National Peking Opera Company, told the official New China News Agency.

The movie's irreverence and creativity are 100 percent American. China remains an authoritarian state run by a party that limits the free flow of information, stifles ingenuity and doesn't understand how to self-correct. Blockbusters don't grow out of the barrel of a gun. Neither do superpowers in the age of globalization.

Yet we overestimate China. Recently I was at a party where a senior aide to a Democratic senator was discussing the business deal [of

2008] in which a Chinese state-owned investment company had bought a chunk of the Blackstone Group, a U.S. investment firm. The Chinese company has lost more than $1 billion, but the aide wouldn't believe it was just a bum investment.

"It's got to be part of a broader plan," she insisted. "It's China." I tried to convince her otherwise. I don't think I succeeded.

EVALUATING THE AUTHOR'S ARGUMENTS:

In this viewpoint John Pomfret suggests that because China's Communist ideology is not attractive to other countries, it is not likely to become a superpower. Explain what he means by this. Then consider American ideologies and products—in what way do you think these have helped it become a superpower?

China's Economic Growth Threatens American Workers

Robert E. Scott

"Growth in trade deficits with China . . . has led to job displacement in all 50 states and the District of Columbia."

In the following viewpoint Robert E. Scott argues that China's economic growth has cost tens of thousands of Americans their jobs. He discusses China's 2001 admittance to the World Trade Organization (WTO), which was supposed to benefit Americans by giving them access to inexpensive goods and services that were produced in accordance with international law. But in reality, says Scott, the deal strengthened China and weakened the United States. Indeed, Chinese wages are much lower than in the United States, and government repression there prevents workers from organizing to win more rights for themselves. As a result, many American manufacturing jobs have been moved to China, where it is cheaper to produce goods. Because they cannot com-

Robert E. Scott, "Costly Trade with China: Millions of U.S. Jobs Displaced with Net Job Loss in Every State," Economic Policy Institute Briefing Paper, October 9, 2007. Reproduced by permission.

pete with such low wages and costs, American companies have slashed jobs, driven down wages, and closed manufacturing plants in all fifty states. The author concludes that American companies should refrain from using Chinese labor and instead push for laws that make American workers more competitive in the global marketplace.

Robert E. Scott is the senior international economist and director of international programs at the Economic Policy Institute, a non-profit, nonpartisan think tank that develops strategies to achieve a fair and prosperous economy. His research focuses on international economics, trade agreements, global finance, and the economic impacts of foreign investment.

AS YOU READ, CONSIDER THE FOLLOWING QUESTIONS:

1. Why is the trade deficit particularly important to employment rates?
2. According to the author, how many jobs have been lost annually in the United States as a result of China's entry into the World Trade Organization in 2001?
3. By what percent have some American manufacturing wages fallen, as reported by Scott?

Contrary to the predictions of its supporters, China's entry into the World Trade Organization (WTO) has failed to reduce its trade surplus with the United States or increase overall U.S. employment. The rise in the U.S. trade deficit with China between 1997 and 2006 has displaced production that could have supported 2,166,000 U.S. jobs. Most of these jobs (1.8 million) have been lost since China entered the WTO in 2001. Between 1997 and 2001, growing trade deficits displaced an average of 101,000 jobs per year, or slightly more than the total employment in Manchester, New Hampshire. Since China entered the WTO in 2001, job losses increased to an average of 353,000 per year—more than the total employment in greater Akron, Ohio. Between 2001 and 2006, jobs were displaced in every state and the District of Columbia. Nearly three-quarters of the jobs displaced were in manufacturing industries. Simply put, the promised benefits of trade liberalization with China have been unfulfilled. . . .

A worker checks new bicycles at a Shanghai bicycle plant. Because Chinese workers earn very low wages, American workers have not been able to compete with them for work.

China's Membership in the WTO Hurts U.S. Workers

China's entry into the WTO was supposed to bring it into compliance with an enforceable, rules-based regime, which would require that it open its markets to imports from the United States and other nations. The United States also negotiated a series of special safeguard measures designed to limit the disruptive effects of surging Chinese imports on domestic producers. However, the core of the agreement failed to include any protections to maintain or improve labor or environmental standards. As a result, China's entry into the WTO has further tilted the international economic playing field against domestic workers and firms, and in favor of multinational companies (MNCs) from the United States and other countries, and state- and privately-owned exporters in China. This has increased the global "race to the bottom" in wages and environmental quality and caused the closing of thousands of U.S. factories, decimating employment in a wide range of communities, states, and entire regions of the United States.

Proponents of China's entry into the WTO frequently claimed that it would create jobs in the United States, increase U.S. exports, and improve the trade deficit with China. President [Bill] Clinton claimed that the agreement allowing China into the WTO, which was negotiated during his administration, "creates a win-win result for both countries". He argued that exports to China "now support hundreds of thousands of American jobs" and that "these figures can grow substantially with the new access to the Chinese market the WTO agreement creates." Others in the White House, such as Kenneth Liberthal, the special advisor to the president and senior director for Asia affairs at the National Security Council, echoed Clinton's assessment:

> Let's be clear as to why a trade deficit might decrease in the short term. China exports far more to the U.S. than it imports [from] the U.S. . . . It will not grow as much as it would have grown without this agreement and over time clearly it will shrink with this agreement.

Promises about jobs and exports misrepresented the real effects of trade on the U.S. economy: trade both creates and destroys jobs. Increases in U.S. exports tend to create jobs in the United States, but increases in imports tend to destroy jobs as imports displace goods that otherwise would have been made in the United States by domestic workers.

Trade with China Destroys U.S. Jobs

The impact of changes in trade on employment is estimated here by calculating the labor content of changes in the trade balance—the difference between exports and imports. Each $1 billion in computer exports to China from the United States supports American jobs. However, each $1 billion in computer imports *from* China displaces those American workers, who would have been employed making them in the United States. On balance, the net employment effect of trade flows depends on the growth in the trade *deficit;* not just exports. Another critically important promise made by the promoters of liberalized U.S.-China trade was that the United States would benefit because of increased exports to a large and growing consumer market in China. This market, in turn, was to be based on an expansion of the middle class that, it was claimed, would grow rapidly due to the wealth created in China by its entry into the WTO. However, the increase in U.S. exports to China has been overwhelmed by the growth of U.S. imports.

The U.S. trade deficit with China has increased from $50 billion in 1997 to $235 billion in 2006, an increase of $185 billion. . . . Between 1997 and 2001, prior to China's entry into the WTO, the deficit increased $9 billion per year on average. Between 2001 and 2006, after China entered the WTO, the deficit increased $30 billion per year on average.

While it is true that exports support jobs in the United States, it is equally true that imports displace them. . . .

U.S. exports to China in 1997 supported 138,000 jobs, but U.S. imports displaced production that would have supported 736,000 jobs. Therefore, the $49 billion trade deficit in 1997 displaced 597,000 jobs in that year. Job displacement rose to 1,000,000 jobs in 2001 and 2,763,000 in 2006. Prior to China's entry into the WTO, an average of 101,000 jobs per year were displaced by growing trade deficits between 1997 and 2001. After 2001, an average of 353,000 jobs per year were lost.

Growing Job Loss

Growth in trade deficits with China has reduced demand for goods produced in every region of the United States and has led to job displacement in all 50 states and the District of Columbia. . . . More than 100,000 jobs were lost in California, Texas, and New York each. Jobs displaced due to growing deficits with China equaled or exceeded 2.0% of total employment in states such as North Carolina and New Hampshire. . . .

Growing trade deficits with China have clearly reduced domestic employment in traded goods industries, especially in the manufacturing sector, which has been hard hit by plant closings and job losses. Workers displaced by trade from the manufacturing sector have been shown to have particular difficulty in securing comparable employment elsewhere in the economy. More than one-third of workers displaced from manufacturing drop out of the labor force. . . . Average wages of those who secured re-employment fell 11% to 13%. Trade-related job displacement pushes many workers out of good jobs in manufacturing and other trade-related industries, often into lower-paying industries and frequently out of the labor market. . . .

Tens of Thousands of Jobs Have Been Lost

Trade with China has cost jobs in every state, mostly in the manufacturing sector.

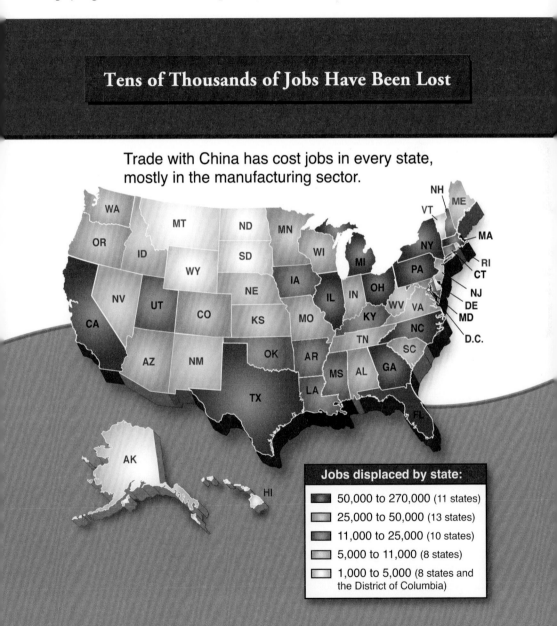

Jobs displaced by state:

- 50,000 to 270,000 (11 states)
- 25,000 to 50,000 (13 states)
- 11,000 to 25,000 (10 states)
- 5,000 to 11,000 (8 states)
- 1,000 to 5,000 (8 states and the District of Columbia)

Taken from: Economic Policy Institute Analysis of Bureau of Labor Statistics and Census Bureau Data.
EPI Briefing Paper #188, October 9, 2007 (Revised).

The U.S.-China Trade Relationship Is Harmful

The growing U.S. trade deficit with China has displaced huge numbers of jobs in the United States, and been a prime contributor to the crisis in manufacturing employment over the past six years. The current U.S.-China trade relationship is bad for both countries. The United States is piling up foreign debt, losing export capacity, and facing a more fragile macroeconomic environment. Meanwhile, China has become dependent on the U.S. consumer market for employment generation, has suppressed the purchasing power of its own middle class with a weak currency, and, most importantly, has held hundreds of billions of hard-currency reserves in low-yielding, risky assets, instead of investing them in public goods that could benefit Chinese households. Its repression of labor rights has suppressed wages, thus subsidizing its exports and making them artificially cheap. This relationship needs a fundamental change: addressing the exchange rate policies and labor standards issues in the Chinese economy are important first steps.

EVALUATING THE AUTHORS' ARGUMENTS:

In the viewpoint you just read, Robert E. Scott explains how trade with China has cost thousands of American workers their jobs. The author of the following viewpoint, James Fallows, paints a very different picture of the U.S.-China trade relationship. How do you account for these differences? With which author do you ultimately agree?

China's Economic Growth Presents Opportunity for American Workers

"Chinese workers making $1,000 a year have been helping American designers, marketers, engineers, and retailers making $1,000 a week (and up) earn even more."

James Fallows

In the following viewpoint James Fallows argues that China's economic growth has provided ample opportunity for American workers. While many American products are made in Chinese factories, the initial conception, marketing, and retailing of the products occur in America. This means that companies need American workers for the engineering, marketing, and retailing of their products. Furthermore, Fallows says the majority of the profits from the sales of products made in China end up in American hands. As such, American workers earn a decent living even when products are manufactured in China. American workers in turn invest the money they earn back into

James Fallows, "China Makes, the World Takes," *The Atlantic Monthly,* July/August 2007. Reproduced by permission of the author.

the American economy by purchasing goods and services from other American workers. The author concludes it is shortsighted to think that jobs in Chinese factories detract from the American economy.

Fallows has served as an editor and a national correspondent for the *Atlantic Monthly* for over twenty-five years and has been chairman of the board for the New America Foundation since 1999. He is also the author of nine books, including *Postcards from Tomorrow Square: Reports from China*.

AS YOU READ, CONSIDER THE FOLLOWING QUESTIONS:
1. What is the "smiley curve," and what does it mean in the context of the viewpoint?
2. What percent of a product's sale price does the author say goes to Chinese factory owners and workers?
3. According to the author, in what ways has China's economic growth benefited American families?

Half the time I have spent in China I have spent in factories. At least that's how it feels—and it's a feeling I sought. The factories where more than 100 million Chinese men and women toil, and from which cameras, clothes, and every other sort of ware flow out to the world, are to me the most startling and intense aspect of today's China. For now, they are also the most important. They are startling above all in their scale. . . . I had no concept of the sweep of what has become the world's manufacturing center: the Pearl River Delta of Guangdong province (the old Canton region), just north of Hong Kong. That one province might have a manufacturing workforce larger than America's. Statistics from China are largely guesses, but Guangdong's population is around 90 million. If even one-fifth of its people hold manufacturing jobs, as seems likely in big cities, that would be 18 million—versus 14 million in the entire United States. . . .

Americans Rely on Goods Made in China

And the factories are important, for China and everyone else. Someday China may matter internationally mainly for the nature of its political system or for its strategic ambitions. Those are significant even now, of course, but China's success in manufacturing is what has determined its place in the world. Most of what has been good about China over the past generation has come directly or indirectly from its factories. The country has public money with which to build roads, houses, and schools—especially roads. The vast population in the countryside has what their forebears acutely lacked, and peasants elsewhere today still do: a chance at paying jobs, which means a chance to escape rural poverty. Americans complain about cheap junk pouring out of Chinese mills, but they rely on China for a lot that is not junk, and whose cheap price is important to American industrial and domestic life. Modern consumer culture rests on the assumption that the nicest, most advanced goods—computers, audio systems, wall-sized TVs—will get cheaper year by year. Moore's Law, which in one version says that the price of computing power will be cut in half every 18 months or so, is part of the reason, but China's factories are a big part too.

Much of what is threatening about today's China also comes from its factories. Many people inside China, and nearly everyone outside, can avoid the direct effects of the country's political controls. It is much harder to avoid its pollution. . . . The heightened competition for oil, ore, and other commodities to feed the factories affects other nations, as do slapdash standards of food purity and

> **FAST FACT**
>
> According to the World Bank, the average annual income in China in 2006 was just $2,025, while the average American annual income was $26,036.

safety, which may have led to tainted worldwide supplies of animal food. The ultimate fear in the developed world, of course, is that as China creates millions of new factory jobs unknown millions will lose such jobs in America, Canada, Germany, even Japan. . . .

China's Growing Economy Benefits Americans

Large-scale shifts in economic power have effects beyond the purely economic. Americans need not be hostile toward China's rise, but they should be wary about its eventual effects. The United States is the only nation with the scale and power to try to set the terms of its interaction with China rather than just succumb. So starting now, Americans need to consider the economic, environmental, political, and social goals they care about defending as Chinese influence grows.

The consideration might best start from the point about which I've changed my mind: So far, America's economic relationship with China has been successful and beneficial—and beneficial for both sides. Free trade may not always be good for all participants, and in the long run trade with China may hold perils for the United States. But based on what I have seen in China, and contrary to what I expected before I came, so far it is working as advertised. Before thinking about what should be changed, Americans should appreciate what has gone right. . . .

Goods Made in China Are Profitable for American Companies

Has the move to China been good for American companies? The answer would seemingly have to be yes—otherwise, why would they go there? It is conceivable that bad partnerships, stolen intellectual property, dilution of brand name, logistics nightmares, or other difficulties have given many companies a sour view of outsourcing; I have heard examples in each category from foreign executives. But the more interesting theme I have heard from them, which explains why they are willing to surmount the inconveniences, involves something called the "smiley curve."

The curve is named for the U-shaped arc of the 1970s-era smiley-face icon, and it runs from the beginning to the end of a product's creation and sale. At the beginning is the company's brand: HP, Siemens, Dell, Nokia, Apple. Next comes the idea for the product: an iPod, a new computer, a camera phone. After that is high-level industrial design—the conceiving of how the product will look and work. Then the detailed engineering design for how it will be made. Then the necessary components. Then the actual manufacture and assembly. Then the shipping and distribution. Then retail sales. And, finally, service contracts and sales of parts and accessories.

The significance is that China's activity is in the middle stages—manufacturing, plus some component supply and engineering

Chinese workers assemble refrigerators in a plant in Qingtao, China. The author argues that cheaply priced products from China are beneficial to American workers.

design—but America's is at the two ends, and those are where the money is. The smiley curve, which shows the profitability or value added at each stage, starts high for branding and product concept, swoops down for manufacturing, and rises again in the retail and servicing stages. The simple way to put this—that the real money is in brand name, plus retail—may sound obvious, but its implications are illuminating.

China Keeps a Small Portion of the Profits

At each factory I visited, I asked managers to estimate how much of a product's sales price ended up in whose hands. The strength of the brand name was the most important variable. If a product is unusual enough and its brand name attractive enough, it could command so high a price that the retailer might keep half the revenue. (Think: an Armani suit, a Starbucks latte.) Most electronics products are now subject to much fiercer price competition, since it is so easy for shoppers to find bargains on the Internet. Therefore the generic Windows-style

China Makes, the U.S. Takes

Each year China produces more and more of the products that are sold in America. This has kept prices low enough for Americans to afford cheap electronics, toys, appliances, and even food.

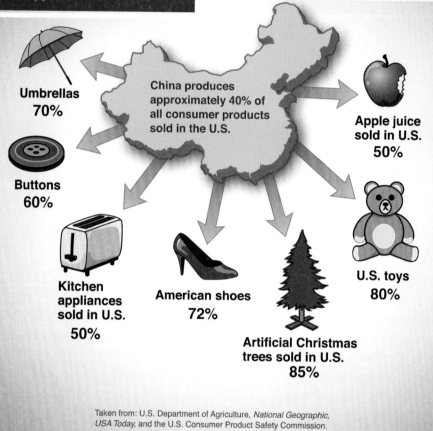

Umbrellas
70%

China produces approximately 40% of all consumer products sold in the U.S.

Apple juice sold in U.S.
50%

Buttons
60%

Kitchen appliances sold in U.S.
50%

American shoes
72%

U.S. toys
80%

Artificial Christmas trees sold in U.S.
85%

Taken from: U.S. Department of Agriculture, *National Geographic*, *USA Today*, and the U.S. Consumer Product Safety Commission.

laptops I saw in one modern factory might go for around $1,000 in the United States, with the retailer keeping less than $50.

Where does the rest of the money go? The manager of that factory guessed that Intel and Microsoft together would collect about $300, and that the makers of the display screen, the disk-storage devices, and other electronic components might get $150 or so apiece. The keyboard makers would get $15 or $20; FedEx or UPS would get slightly less. When all other costs were accounted for, perhaps $30 to \$40—3 to 4 percent of the total—would stay in China with the factory owners and the young women on the assembly lines.

Other examples: A carrying case for an audio device from a big-name Western company retails for just under \$30. That company pays the Chinese supplier \$6 per case, of which about half goes for materials. The other \$24 stays with the big-name company. An earphone-like accessory for another U.S.-brand audio device also retails for about \$30. Of this, I was told, \$3 stayed in China. . . .

Chinese Factories Support American Jobs

In case the point isn't clear: Chinese workers making \$1,000 a year have been helping American designers, marketers, engineers, and retailers making \$1,000 a week (and up) earn even more. Plus, they have helped shareholders of U.S.-based companies.

All this is apart from [another] phenomenon . . . : China's conversion of its trade surpluses into a vast hoard of dollar-denominated reserves. Everyone understands that in the short run China's handling of its reserves has been a convenience to the United States. By placing more than \$1 trillion in U.S. stock and bond markets, it has propped up the U.S. economy. Asset prices are higher than they would otherwise be; interest rates are lower, whether for American families taking out mortgages or for American taxpayers financing the ever-mounting federal debt. The dollar has also fallen less than it otherwise would have—which in the short run helps American consumers keep buying Chinese goods.

Everyone also understands that in the long run China must change this policy. Its own people need too many things—schools, hospitals, railroads—for it to keep sending its profits to America. . . .

America Needs to Adjust Its Attitude Toward China

American complaints about the RMB [yuan renminbi, Chinese currency], about subsidies, and about other Chinese practices have this in common: They assume that the solution to long-term tensions in the trading relationship lies in changes on China's side. I think that assumption is naive. If the United States is unhappy with the effects of its interaction with China, that's America's problem, not China's. To imagine that the United States can stop China from pursuing its own economic ambitions through nagging, threats, or enticement is to fool ourselves. If a country does not like the terms of its business dealings with the world, it needs to change its own policies, not expect the world to change. China has done just that, to its own benefit—and, up until now, to America's.

Are we uncomfortable with the America that is being shaped by global economic forces? The inequality? The sense of entitlement for some? Of stifled opportunity for others? The widespread fear that today's trends—borrowing, consuming, looking inward, using up infrastructure—will make it hard to stay ahead tomorrow, particularly in regard to China? If so, those trends themselves, and the American choices behind them, are what Americans can address. They're not China's problem, and they're not the fault of anyone in Shenzhen.

EVALUATING THE AUTHOR'S ARGUMENTS:

In the viewpoint you just read, James Fallows uses history, facts, and examples to make his argument that China's economic success has not eliminated American jobs. He does not, however, use any quotations to support his point. If you were to rewrite this article and insert quotations, what authorities might you quote from? Where would you place these quotations to bolster the points Fallows makes?

China Poses a Military Threat to the United States

John J. Tkacik Jr.

"China's intent is to challenge the United States as a military superpower."

In the following viewpoint John J. Tkacik Jr. argues that China poses a military threat to the United States. He explains how, in recent years, China has spent millions of dollars modernizing its navy, air force, and space program. It has also built more and more planes, submarines, and long-range ballistic missiles, which have greatly increased its ability to wage war. Tkacik says that while the United States was once the world's military leader in terms of size and ability, China now threatens America's dominance. He concludes that Americans should fear China's military buildup and warns that China will one day challenge the United States politically and militarily.

Tkacik is a senior researcher at the Heritage Foundation. He is also a retired diplomat who served overseas with the U.S. Foreign Service in Taiwan, Hong Kong, and China. He is the author of *Rethinking One China*, a book about U.S. policy toward China and Taiwan.

John J. Tkacik Jr., "A Chinese Military Superpower?" The Heritage Foundation, March 8, 2007. Reproduced by permission.

AS YOU READ, CONSIDER THE FOLLOWING QUESTIONS:
1. According to the author, how much did China spend on its military in 2007?
2. How many submarines does Tkacik say China has added to its navy?
3. Name at least three ways in which the author reports China has improved its air and space abilities.

On March 4 [2007], China's National People's Congress announced that it would increase the country's military budget 17.8 percent in 2007 to a total of $45 billion. Despite the fact that this was the biggest single annual increase in China's military spending, the Chinese government reassured the world that this spending hike was normal and need not worry anyone. "China is committed to taking a path of peaceful development and it pursues a defensive military posture," a spokesman said. But the evidence suggests instead that China's intent is to challenge the United States as a military superpower.

China's Military Spending Has Increased

A closer look at China's military spending raises profound questions about China's geopolitical direction. In terms of purchasing power parity (PPP), China's effective military spending is far greater than $45 billion, or even the U.S. Department of Defense's $105 billion estimate. In fact, it is in the $450 billion range, putting it in the same league as the United States and far ahead of any other country, including Russia. This figure reflects the reality that a billion dollars can buy a lot more "bang" in China than in the United States.

Within a decade, perhaps much sooner, China will be America's only global competitor for military and strategic influence. Director of National Intelligence Michael McConnell told the Senate on February 27 [2007] that the Chinese are "building their military, in my view, to reach some state of parity with the United States," adding that "they're a threat today, they would become an increasing threat over time." Nor is this a revelation to Washington policy-makers. McConnell's predecessor John Negroponte testified to the Senate Intelligence

Committee in February 2006 that "China is a rapidly rising power with steadily expanding global reach that may become a peer competitor to the United States at some point." In June 2005, Secretary of State Condoleezza Rice observed that the U.S. must help integrate China into the international, rules-based economy before it becomes a "military superpower." Rice, with a doctorate in Soviet studies and years of experience in the White House during the last days of the Cold War, would not use the term "superpower" lightly.

It remains to be seen whether China's now massive stake in the global economy will result in Beijing becoming a responsible stakeholder in global affairs, but Beijing seems poised for true global status as a "military superpower." The latest figures from the econometricians at the Central Intelligence Agency—whose data come from the World Bank—peg China's 2006 GDP [gross domestic product], adjusted for purchasing power parity, at $10 trillion, with a nominal exchange-rate value of $2.5 trillion.

Chinese soldiers perform maneuvers in Inner Mongolia in September 2008. The author argues that China's expanding military poses a real threat to the United States.

Evidence of a Growing Military

Despite the Chinese Communist Party leadership's espousal of China's "peaceful rise," the unprecedented peacetime expansion of China's military capabilities betrays a clear intent to challenge the United States in the Western Pacific and establish itself as the region's predominant military power. With China's massive GDP and military spending at an estimated 4.5 percent of GDP, the resources that Beijing now devotes to its armed forces surely make it a top global power. The exact methodology that U.S. intelligence agencies use to arrive at this estimate is classified, but it reportedly takes into account the fact that China's budget figures do not include foreign arms purchases, subsidies to military industries, any of China's space program (which is under the command of the Central Military Commission), or the costs of the 660,000 strong "People's Armed Police." It appears that some defense spending sectors that are not counted in the defense budget have increased much faster than the budget itself.

At a time when The Heritage Foundation is encouraging sustained U.S. defense spending of 4 percent of GDP in an initiative called "Four Percent for Freedom," China's military budget could be called "Four-and-a-Half Percent Against Freedom" due to its involvement in countries like Burma, Sudan, Zimbabwe, North Korea, Uzbekistan, and Iran, not to mention its actions against freedom in Taiwan and, of course, in China itself.

U.S. intelligence agencies can plainly see where the money is going. China is assembling a blue-water navy, with a submarine fleet of 29 modern boats, including 13 super-quiet Russian-made Kilo class subs and 14 Chinese-made Song and Yuan class diesel electric submarines that are reportedly improved versions of the Kilos. At least 10 more of these submarines are in China's shipyards, together with five

China's Defense Budget

China increases its military spending every year and usually spends more than it announces to the public.

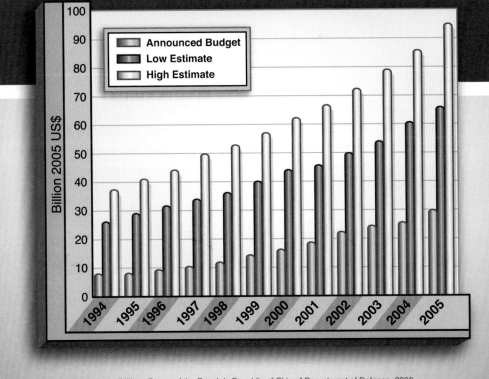

Taken from: "Military Power of the People's Republic of China," Department of Defense, 2006.

new nuclear ballistic missile and attack boats. China's surface fleet is also undergoing a similar modernization.

China's Air and Space Power

China's power in the air and in space is also on the rise. The People's Liberation Army (PLA) Air Force has about 300 Russian-designed fourth-generation Sukhoi-27 Flankers and a number of Chinese-built *Jian*-11 planes and 76 Sukhoi-30 multi-role jets. With Russian and Israeli assistance, the PLA Air Force has acquired an additional 50 or so *Jian*-10 fighters based on U.S. F-16 technology and reportedly plans to build 250 more. China's rocket forces are also expanding at an unprec-

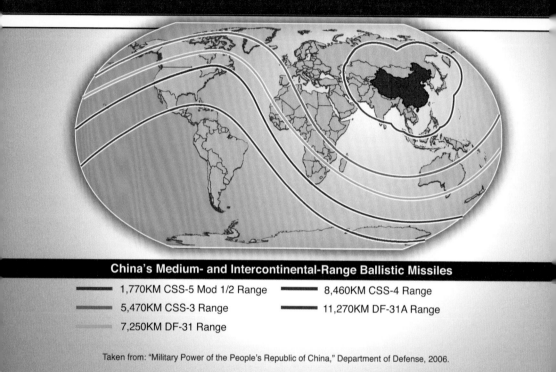

China's Military Reach

China currently is capable of targeting its nuclear forces throughout the region and most of the world, including the continental United States.

China's Medium- and Intercontinental-Range Ballistic Missiles

- 1,770KM CSS-5 Mod 1/2 Range
- 5,470KM CSS-3 Range
- 7,250KM DF-31 Range
- 8,460KM CSS-4 Range
- 11,270KM DF-31A Range

Taken from: "Military Power of the People's Republic of China," Department of Defense, 2006.

edented pace, with production and deployment of short-range ballistic missiles targeted at Taiwan increasing from 50 per year during the 1990s to between 100 and 150 per year today. Presumably, output from Chinese ICBM [intercontinental ballistic missile] factories is expanding at a similar pace. Most recently, China's January 12 [2007] test of highly sophisticated direct-ascent "kinetic kill vehicle" (KKV) technology, coupled with attempts to blind or laser-illuminate a U.S. reconnaissance satellite in 2006, are convincing evidence of the PLA's intention to neutralize the United States' military assets in space in any conflict.

A Military Superpower in the Making

Indeed, China's 2006 "White Paper" on national defense describes a China that is moving onto the offensive:

The Army aims at moving *from regional defense to trans-regional mobility*, and improving its capabilities in air-ground integrated operations, *long-distance maneuvers*, rapid assaults and special operations. The Navy aims at gradual extension of the strategic depth for offshore defensive operations and enhancing its capabilities in integrated maritime operations and nuclear counterattacks. The Air Force aims at speeding up its transition from territorial air defense to both *offensive* and defensive operations, and increasing its capabilities in the areas of air strike, air and missile defense, early warning and reconnaissance, and *strategic projection*. The Second Artillery Force aims at progressively improving its force structure of having both nuclear and conventional missiles, and raising its capabilities in strategic deterrence and conventional strike under conditions of informationization.

The ultimate question must be whether Beijing's leaders have any purpose in assembling a military machine worthy of a superpower other than to have the strength to challenge the United States' strategic position in Asia. It is time to take China's military expansion seriously.

EVALUATING THE AUTHORS' ARGUMENTS:

In this viewpoint John J. Tkacik Jr. warns that China's increased military spending has created a modern military that can directly compete with the U.S. military. The author of the following viewpoint, Henry Rosemont Jr., argues that despite increased spending, China's military is in no way equivalent to the U.S. military. With which author's perspective do you agree? Why?

China Does Not Pose a Military Threat to the United States

Henry Rosemont Jr.

"The Chinese have much better grounds for fearing the United States than the other way around."

In the following viewpoint Henry Rosemont Jr. argues that China does not pose a military threat to the United States. He explains that China does not have a sophisticated-enough military to compete with the United States—it lacks technically advanced equipment, skilled manpower, and the international influence needed to hold such a position. It would take technology, money, and manpower that China does not have to even come close to competing with the United States, says the author. Furthermore, China knows if it were to attack the United States, it would quickly be obliterated. Without an advanced military, China is currently not a threat to the United States or any other potential superpower, the author concludes.

Rosemont is a contributor to Foreign Policy in Focus, a think tank for the Institute of Policy Studies that analyzes U.S. foreign policy and international affairs and recom-

Henry Rosemont Jr., "Is China a Threat?" Foreign Policy in Focus, February 7, 2008. Reproduced by permission.

mends alternatives to current policies. He also is professor emeritus at St. Mary's College of Maryland and a visiting scholar in the religious studies department at Brown University.

AS YOU READ, CONSIDER THE FOLLOWING QUESTIONS:
1. Why are China's soldiers no match for U.S. soldiers, according to the author?
2. How many of the world's twenty-one aircraft carriers does the author say belong to China?
3. According to the author, how many nuclear weapons does China have? How many does the United States have?

China's unprecedented industrial growth over the last two decades has raised the question of whether it now poses a threat to the security of the United States economically, militarily, or both. Economically, the extent to which China truly threatens the United States depends at least in part on the chauvinistic assumption that *any* potential challenge to absolute U.S. global economic dominance is threatening.

On the military question, the answer is much clearer. China is not a military threat to the United States. Only those who believe that Fu Manchu [a fictional character known for being an evil criminal genius] is alive and well in the Middle Kingdom and fulfilling his dreams of world domination through a large and aggressive army, air force, and navy still subscribe to a notion that China poses a global military threat. Several recent books on the Chinese military perpetuate this myth. Their titles reveal everything: *Imagined Enemies: China Prepares for Uncertain War*, for instance, or *Showdown: Why China Wants War with the United States*.

These and numerous similar narratives share an alarmist tone combined with a dearth of relevant facts in support of their claims. These books suffer from such flaws for good reason. The facts belie the claims, especially when placed in comparative perspective. When it comes to the putative Chinese military threat, the numbers simply don't add up.

The author argues that one of the reasons China should not be viewed as a threat is that most of its planes are over forty years old and obsolete.

China's Military Is No Match for the United States

Much has been made of the double-digit increase in Chinese defense spending [since 2005]. China has indeed increased its spending. But much of the additional expenditures have been devoted to upgrading information, weapons, and communications systems. At the same, China has cut troop strength to almost half of what it was in 1990. Moreover, the estimate of military expenditures for 2006 is $35 billion. That is about 7% of the U.S. defense budget, once the costs of the wars in Iraq and Afghanistan are factored in. Even before including these latter expenditures the U.S. military budget is now larger than the defense budgets of all other nations *combined*. Almost surely China's actual military expenditures are larger than the 2006 estimate. But even if the military budget is twice as large, $70 billion is still less than 15% of the U.S. total and less than what was spent in Iraq and Afghanistan [in 2007] alone.

In terms of ground forces, the People's Liberation Army (PLA) has an active duty component of 2.3 million personnel. That's a lot of soldiers, but the United States has 1.4 million, with less than one-fourth of the population. True, the Chinese have reserve forces of another million plus. But they are responsible, among other things, for patrolling more than 8,000 miles of borders with India and Russia—not always the friendliest of neighbors in the past—functions the U.S. military does not perform at the Canadian and Mexican borders. Moreover, despite the supply breakdown scandal in Iraq, the 1.4 million U.S. troops are much better equipped overall than their Chinese counterparts, few of whom have state-of-the-art support materiel or personal safety equipment.

The PLA's air force capabilities, meanwhile, are no match in quality for the United States either defensively or offensively. Many of China's aircraft models are over 40 years old. . . .

China's Navy Is Weak

China's weakest link is naval. It has no blue ocean navy [a navy capable of operating in open seas] and it is difficult to imagine how it could dream of building one. Of the 21 large aircraft carriers operational in the world right now, 12 are American, with a total landing space of 75 acres. The carriers belonging to the rest of the world have 15 acres altogether. *None* of the other aircraft carriers belongs to China. So, the score is rather lopsided on the naval front: the United States 12, China 0.

The picture is similar for submarines. In a 2005 *Atlantic Monthly* article Robert Kaplan issued the dire warning that "The Middle East is just a blip. The American military contest with China in the Pacific will define the 21st century. And China will be a more formidable adversary than Russia ever was." Kaplan cites as one important piece of "evidence" supporting his doom and gloom scenarios the fact that "The Chinese are investing in both diesel-powered and nuclear-powered submarines—*a clear signal* that they intend not only to protect their coasts but also to *expand their influence far out into the Pacific*." [Italics added.]

In the first place, the Chinese might have a hard time "expanding their influence far out into the Pacific" because so many U.S. soldiers,

FAST FACT

According to a 2007 UPI-Zogby International poll, only 7.2 percent of Americans believe China represents a military threat to the United States.

sailors, marines, and air force personnel are already stationed in the region. There are 18,000 troops stationed in Alaska, 60,000 in Hawaii, 37,000 in Japan, 5,000 on Guam, and 30,000 in South Korea. Again, the Chinese number is zero. The United States has over 700 military installations outside its borders overall, while the Chinese have none at present.

China's Military Influence Is Not Expanding

Kaplan's supposedly "clear signal" of expansion rests on the fact that the Chinese already have 55 submarines, and have a few more under construction. But 50 of these are diesel-powered and hence must surface or near-surface every few days to take in oxygen. This makes them more vulnerable to detection and destruction (by U.S. reconnaissance satellites and missile launchers) than nuclear submarines. Although formidable vessels, these diesel submarines are in the end not even a secure *defense* against the highly sophisticated technology of the world's sole superpower, let alone a military threat to it. Strictly in terms of deterrence, then, it is unsurprising that the Chinese would like more nuclear-powered submarines than the five that are currently operational for protecting their shores.

On the other hand, the United States currently has 72 submarines, *all* of which are nuclear-powered. And more are on the way, including the Virginia-class attack submarine, not a vessel designed for defense. Perhaps most frightening for the Chinese are the U.S. underwater capabilities in the Pacific, where the Navy maintains two-thirds of its strategic submarine forces. "At least 2 of these submarines are kept on "hard alert" in the Pacific at all times, meaning they're ready to fire within 15 minutes of a launch order," write Keir Lieber and Daryl Press. "Since each submarine carries 24 nuclear-tipped missiles with an average of six warheads per missile, commanders have almost 300 warheads ready for immediate use. This is more than enough to assign multiple warheads to each of the 18 silos in which the Chinese have nuclear missiles capable of reaching the US. Chinese leaders would have little or no warning of the attack."

Finally, China has 100–400 nuclear weapons. But only the 18 in the silos mentioned above are capable of striking the western continental United States and these cannot be launched quickly. Unless fired as a first-strike weapon, they could easily be destroyed. The

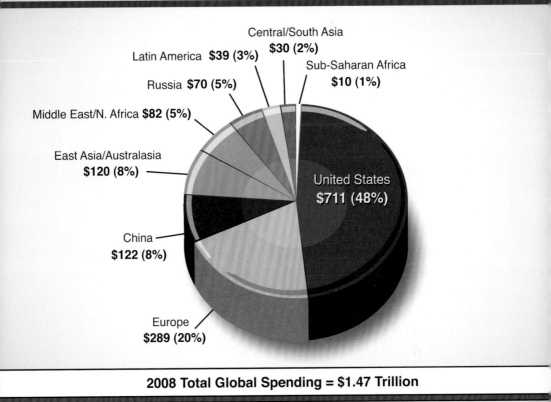

This pie chart shows military spending in billions (U.S. dollars), with percent of total global spending.

Central/South Asia
$30 (2%)

Latin America $39 (3%)

Sub-Saharan Africa
$10 (1%)

Russia $70 (5%)

Middle East/N. Africa $82 (5%)

East Asia/Australasia
$120 (8%)

United States
$711 (48%)

China
$122 (8%)

Europe
$289 (20%)

2008 Total Global Spending = $1.47 Trillion

Taken from: The Center for Arms Control and Non-Proliferation. www.armscontrolcenter.org.

United States, on the other hand, has almost 10,000 nuclear warheads and sufficient delivery capabilities to obliterate every Chinese city with a population of a half-million or more, and still have more than enough of a stockpile to hold the rest of the world at bay.

It Is Not in China's Best Interests to Expand Its Military

It should thus be clear that the Chinese have much better grounds for fearing the United States than the other way around, and this holds true not only in terms of actual military capabilities, but also in the readiness and willingness to use them. Unlike the United States, which has well over a quarter of a million troops stationed overseas with attendant army, naval, and air force weapons and delivery systems equal to the rest of the world together, the entire Chinese army, navy, and air force are based within its own borders, and shooting at no one.

Absent future U.S. provocation, the Chinese will not likely try to match the United States militarily as the former Soviet Union did.

EVALUATING THE AUTHORS' ARGUMENTS:

In the viewpoint you just read, Henry Rosemont Jr. argues that China is nowhere near close to building a military superpower on par with the United States'. In the previous viewpoint, John J. Tkacik Jr. argues that it is. After reading both viewpoints, with which author do you agree? List at least three pieces of evidence that swayed you.

Facts About China

Editor's note: These facts can be used in reports or papers to reinforce or add credibility when making important points or claims.

According to the U.S. State Department:

- The population of China is nearly five times that of the United States.
- China has fifty-six ethnic groups, with Han accounting for 92 percent of the total population of 1.3 billion.
- The remaining 8 percent are Zhuang (16 million), Manchu (10 million), Hui (9 million), Miao (8 million), Uygur (7 million), Yi (7 million), Mongolian (5 million), Tibetan (5 million), Buyi (3 million), Korean (2 million), and other ethnic minorities.
- China has an estimated population growth rate of about 0.6 percent.
- Chinese law permits just one child per family, with allowance for a second child under certain circumstances, especially in rural areas, and with guidelines looser for ethnic minorities with small populations.
- The Chinese population is expected to peak at around 1.6 billion by 2050.
- There are seven major Chinese dialects and many subdialects.
- Mandarin (or Putonghua), the predominant dialect, is spoken by over 70 percent of the population.
- Mandarin is taught in all schools and is the dialect of the government.
- About two-thirds of the Han ethnic group are native speakers of Mandarin; the rest, concentrated in southwest and southeast China, speak one of the six other major Chinese dialects.
- Though China is an officially atheist country, Buddhism is widely practiced. Official estimates claim there are 100 million Buddhists, 20 million Muslims, 15 million Protestants, and 5 million Catholics; unofficial estimates are much higher, however.

China's Economy
According to the World Bank:
- In 1985 average annual income in China was $293; in 2006 the average annual income was $2,025.
- About 20 percent of China's exports go to the United States.
- China contributed one-third of global economic growth in 2004.
- In 2004 China accounted for half of global growth in metals demand and one-third global growth in oil demand.

According to the International Energy Agency, China's gross domestic product, measured in purchasing power parity, will exceed that of the United States by 2020.

According to *National Geographic:*
- China will overtake the United States as the world's largest economy in ten years.
- Urban Chinese earn more than three times as much as those in rural areas.
- The number of cell phones has grown in China from 87 million in 2000 to 432 million today.

China and Energy
According to the International Energy Agency:
- China will become the world's top consumer of energy, surpassing the United States, in the first few years of the next decade (from 2010 to 2012).
- China became a net importer of coal in 2007; in 2030 it will account for nearly half of world coal consumption.
- China will quadruple its oil imports between 2006 and 2030.
- China's total carbon dioxide emissions are expected to exceed those of the United States in 2008.
- China will be responsible for 62 percent of the increase in world coal consumption by 2030.
- China's oil imports in 2030 (which will be 13.1 million barrels per day) will be similar to those of the United States and the European Union in 2006 (13.6 million and 13.5 million barrels per day, respectively).
- In 2005, 8.5 million Chinese lived without electricity.

According to the *American Chronicle:*
- China is the world's largest producer of hydropower, the use of moving water to generate power.
- Six percent of China's energy needs are met by hydropower, and the nation only uses one-fourth of its current potential.
- China has eighty-seven thousand dams.
- The largest dam in the world is China's Three Gorges Dam, which cost $30 billion to build and which displaced more than 1 million people.
- China's demand for energy is expected to grow at a rate of 6 percent annually.
- Over 75 percent of China's energy is supplied by coal.
- By 2025, 77 percent of China's oil supplies will be imported.
- China's consumption of coal is expected to supply 78 percent of power demand until 2030.
- China is the world's second-largest consumer of energy after the United States and was its third-largest energy producer.
- China is the fifth-largest oil-producing nation on Earth, with proven reserves of around 16 billion barrels.
- In 2006 the Chinese government pledged to make renewable energy account for 15 percent of the country's energy needs by 2020. It has pledged to cut coal use by 13 percent by that year.

According to *National Geographic:*
- One thousand new cars are added to roads in China every day.
- China has the number of cars per capita that the United States did in 1915.
- There are 9 privately owned cars per every 1,000 Chinese residents; in the United States, there are 450 privately owned cars per every 1,000 residents.
- Thirty-seven percent of Chinese drivers did not know how to drive three years ago.
- The death rate from car accidents is 4.5 times higher in China than in the United States.
- If all the Chinese expressways slated for completion by the end of 2008 were lined up, they would circle the equator 1.5 times.
- There are expected to be 115 McDonald's drive-thrus in China by the end of 2008, compared with just 1 in 2005.

China and Pollution

The World Bank reports:

- Twenty of the top 30 polluted cities in the world are located in China.
- China has the world's highest number of annual deaths triggered by air pollution.
- Seven hundred fifty thousand people die prematurely every year in China from pollution-related disease.
- About sixty thousand people die prematurely from diarrhea and cancers caused by polluted water in rural areas.

China and the Internet

Chinese Internet use has exploded since 2004:

- In 2004 there were 94 million Chinese Internet users.
- In 2005 there were 111 million Chinese Internet users.
- In 2006 there were 137 million Chinese Internet users.
- In 2007 there were 210 million Chinese Internet users.
- In 2008 there were 253 million Chinese Internet users.

China now surpasses the United States, which has about 220 million online users.

The percentage of American Internet users continues to be much greater than in China: 71 percent of the American population is online, compared to 17 percent of China's.

A poll conducted by the Pew Internet & American Life Project from 2000–2007 found the following opinions on Chinese Internet censorship:

- More than 80 percent of Chinese citizens think the Internet should be managed or controlled in some way.
- Eighty-seven percent of Internet users would want pornography controlled or managed.
- Eighty-six percent would want violent content controlled or managed.
- Eighty-three percent would want spam or junk mail controlled or managed.

- Sixty-six percent would want advertisements controlled or managed.
- Sixty-four percent would want slander against individuals controlled or managed.
- Fifty percent would want online gaming controlled or managed.
- Forty-one percent would want online political content controlled or managed.
- Twenty-seven percent would want online chatting controlled or managed.
- Eighty-five percent believe the Chinese government should be responsible for controlling or managing online content.
- Seventy-nine percent said Internet companies should be responsible for controlling or managing online content.
- Sixty-eight percent said parents should be responsible for controlling or managing online content.
- Sixty-four percent said schools should be responsible for controlling or managing online content.
- Fifty-nine percent said Internet cafés should be responsible for controlling or managing online content.

Organizatons to Contct

The editors have compiled the following list of organizations concerned with the issues debated in this book. The descriptions are derived from materials provided by the organizations. All have publications or information available for interested readers. The list was compiled on the date of publication of the present volume; the information provided here may change. Be aware that many organizations take several weeks or longer to respond to queries, so allow as much time as possible.

American Enterprise Institute (AEI)
1150 Seventeenth St. NW
Washington, DC 20036
(202) 862-5800
e-mail: VRodman@aei.org
Web site: www.aei.org

The institute is a public policy research organization dedicated to preserving and strengthening government, private enterprise, foreign policy, and national defense. Its Asian Studies Program focuses on the growing offensive capabilities of China's army, relations between Taiwan and mainland China, and economic and political reform in China. AEI's magazine, *American Enterprise*, often deals with developments in Asia, and the institute also publishes several books on China.

Amnesty International (AI)
5 Penn Plaza, 6th Ave.
New York, NY 10001
(212) 807-8400
e-mail: admin-us@aiusa.org
Web site: www.amnesty.org

This international organization works to promote human rights around the world. In 1999 it launched the "China: Ten Years After Tiananmen" campaign to raise awareness of the imprisonment of political dissidents in China. Details of the campaign are available on the group's Web site.

AI also publishes an annual report detailing human rights violations in many countries, including China.

The Asia Society
725 Park Ave.
New York, NY 10021
(212) 288-6400
Web site: www.asiasociety.org

The Asia Society is an educational organization dedicated to fostering understanding of Asia and communication between Americans and the peoples of Asia and the Pacific. Reports and articles about China are available on its Web site.

Brookings Institution
1775 Massachusetts Ave. NW
Washington, DC 20036
(202) 797-6000
Web site: www.brookings.org

Founded in 1927, the institution conducts research and analyzes global events and their impact on the United Sates and U.S. foreign policy. It publishes the quarterly *Brookings Review* as well as numerous books and research papers on foreign policy, many of which feature China.

Cato Institute
1000 Massachusetts Ave. NW
Washington, DC 20001-5403
(202) 842-0200
Web site: www.cato.org

The Cato Institute is a nonpartisan public policy research foundation that promotes the principles of limited government, individual liberty, and peace. Relations with China are a major research area within the institute's division of foreign policy studies. The institute regularly publishes policy analysis reports and op-eds that focus on foreign policy and trade issues involving China.

Center for Security Policy (CSP)
1901 Pennsylvania Ave. NW, Ste. 201
Washington, DC 20006

(202) 835-9077
Web site: www.security-policy.org

The Center for Security Policy's mission is to stimulate debate about all aspects of security policy, notably those policies regarding the foreign, defense, economic, financial, and technology interests of the United States. It believes that China poses a threat to U.S. national security and warns of this in many of its press releases and position papers.

Center for Strategic and International Studies (CSIS)
1800 K St. NW, Ste. 400
Washington, DC 20006
(202) 887-0200
fax: (202) 775-3199
Web site: www.csis.org

The center works to provide world leaders with strategic insights and policy options on current and emerging global issues. It publishes the *Washington Quarterly*, a journal on political, economic, and security issues, and other publications that frequently focus on China. Reports can be downloaded from its Web site.

Council on Foreign Relations
58 E. Sixty-eighth St.
New York, NY 10021
(212) 434-9400
fax: (212) 434-9800
e-mail: communications@cfr.org
Web site: www.cfr.org

The council researches the international aspects of American economic and political policies. Its journal *Foreign Affairs*, published five times a year, provides analysis on global situations, including those pertaining to China.

Freedom House
1301 Connecticut Ave. NW, Floor 6
Washington, DC 20036
(202) 296-5101
e-mail: info@freedomhouse.org
Web site: www.freedomhouse.org

Freedom House promotes human rights, democracy, free market economics, the rule of law, and independent media around the world. It publishes *Freedom in the World*, an annual comparative assessment of the state of political rights and civil liberties in 191 countries. Freedom House consistently ranks China as Not Free, and it publishes other reports and articles about the status of human rights in that country.

Heritage Foundation
214 Massachusetts Ave. NE
Washington, DC 20002-4999
(202) 546-4400
e-mail: info@heritage.org
Web site: www.heritage.org

The Heritage Foundation is a conservative think tank that formulates and promotes public policies based on the principles of free enterprise, limited government, individual freedom, traditional American values, and a strong national defense. It publishes many position papers on U.S.-China policy, such as "How Trade with China Benefits Americans" and "Time to Act on Taiwan's Security."

Hoover Institution
434 Galvez Mall
Stanford University
Stanford, CA 94305-6010
(650) 723-1754
e-mail: horaney@hoover.stanford.edu
Web site: www.hoover.org

The Hoover Institution is a public policy research center housed at Stanford University. It is devoted to advanced study of politics, economics, and political economy—both domestic and foreign—as well as international affairs. It publishes the quarterly *Hoover Digest*, which often includes articles on China, as well as a newsletter.

Human Rights in China (HRIC)
350 Fifth Ave., Ste. 3311
New York, NY 10118
(212) 239-4495

e-mail: hrichina@hrichina.org
Web site: www.hrichina.org

HRIC is an international nongovernmental organization founded by Chinese scientists and scholars. It monitors the implementation of international human rights standards in the People's Republic of China and carries out human rights advocacy and education among Chinese people inside and outside the country. HRIC's publications include the *China Rights Forum*, as well as books, recordings, and reports on the status of human rights in China.

Human Rights Watch
350 Fifth Ave., 34th Floor
New York, NY 10118-3299
(212) 290-4700
e-mail: hrwnyc@hrw.org
Web site: www.hrw.org

Human Rights Watch is an international advocacy organization whose goal is to raise awareness about human rights and to investigate and expose human rights violations. It publishes annual reports about human rights around the world as well as special reports on China's treatment of its citizens and the people of Taiwan.

Institute for Policy Studies
1112 Sixteenth St. NW, Ste. 600
Washington, DC 20036
(202) 234-9382
e-mail: info@ips-dc.org

The goal of the Institute for Policy Studies is to empower people to build healthy and democratic societies in communities, the United States, and around the world. They are the publishers of *Foreign Policy in Focus* (www.fpif.org), which offers briefings and reports on major developments in U.S. foreign policy regarding China.

Laogai Research Foundation
1109 M St. NW
Washington, DC 20005
(202) 408-8301

e-mail: laogai@laogai.org
Web site: www.laogai.org

The foundation is dedicated to collecting information about China's system of forced-labor camps. Its publications include the *Laogai Handbook* and the report *Killing by Quota, Killing for Profit: Executions and Transplants in China.*

The National Endowment for Democracy (NED)
1101 Fifteenth St. NW, Ste. 700
Washington, DC 20005
(202) 293-9072
fax: (202) 223-6042
e-mail: info@ned.org

The National Endowment for Democracy (NED) is a private, non-profit organization created in 1983 to strengthen democratic institutions around the world through nongovernmental efforts. It publishes the bimonthly periodical *Journal of Democracy.*

For Further Reading

Books

Bongiorni, Sara. *A Year Without "Made in China": One Family's True Life Adventure in the Global Economy.* New York: Wiley, 2008. A writer's story of trying to live for a year without buying any products made in China.

Fishman, Ted C. *China, Inc.: How the Rise of the Next Superpower Challenges America and the World.* New York: Scribner, 2006. Details how hundreds of millions of peasants have migrated from rural to urban areas to find manufacturing jobs, providing an unlimited, low-wage workforce to power China's economy. In the process, this shift has changed both Chinese culture and the global business climate in significant ways.

Kynge, James. *China Shakes the World: A Titan's Rise and Troubled Future—and the Challenge for America.* New York: Mariner, 2007. Written by a former bureau chief of the *Financial Times*, this book demonstrates how China's thirst for jobs, raw materials, energy, and new markets—and its export of goods, workers, and investments—will dramatically reshape world trade and politics.

Mann, James. *The China Fantasy: How Our Leaders Explain Away Chinese Repression.* New York: Viking, 2007. Criticizes American leaders for communicating to the public in a soothing but dangerously misleading way about China.

Meredith, Robyn. *The Elephant and the Dragon: The Rise of India and China and What It Means for All of Us.* New York: Norton, 2008. Argues that the United States should not fear these two rising economic powers.

Navarro, Peter. *The Coming China Wars: Where They Will Be Fought and How They Can Be Won.* Upper Saddle River, New Jersey: FT, 2008. Describes an emerging power beleaguered by both internal and external threats.

Periodicals

Associated Press. "China Blocks YouTube After Videos of Tibet Protests Are Posted," *New York Times*, March 17, 2008.

Branstetter, Lee, and Nicholas Lardy. "China's Embrace of Globalization," NBER Working Paper No. 12373, July 2006.

Cody, Edward. "China's Patchy Tibet Blackout," *Washington Post*, March 20, 2008.

Collier, Robert. "China on Global Hunt to Quench Its Thirst for Oil," *San Francisco Chronicle*, June 26, 2005.

Dyer, Geoff. "China Plays Down Fears over Product Safety at Home," *Financial Times*, August 22, 2007.

Economist. "Blood Debts: AIDS in China," January 20, 2007.

French, Howard W. "Despite Flaws, Rights in China Have Expanded," *New York Times*, August 2, 2008.

Halloran, Richard. "China's Paths to Hegemony," *Washington Times*, January 17, 2008.

Harris, Shane. "China's Cyber-Militia," *National Journal*, May 31, 2008.

Huang, Gregory T. "Boys From the Wang Ba: The Chinese Are Moving Online in Droves, and It's Changing the Face of the Internet," *New Scientist*, November 10, 2007.

International Crisis Group. "China's Thirst for Oil," *Asia Report*, June 9, 2008. www.crisisgroup.org/library/documents/asia/153_china_s_thirst_for_oil.pdf.

Kwong, Robin. "China's Billionaires Begin to Add Up," *Financial Times*, October 23, 2007.

LaFranchi, Howard. "China's Human Rights Rating Upgraded by U.S. State Dept.," *Christian Science Monitor*, March 13, 2008.

Larmer, Brook. "Bitter Waters: Can China Save the Yellow—Its Mother River?" *National Geographic*, May 2008.

Lee, Ellen. "A Web of Change; More Openness: Internet Eroding Government Grip on Information," *San Francisco Chronicle*, August 5, 2008.

Levy, Philip I. "When Form Follows Function: China's Property Pangs," *TCS Daily*, March 20, 2007.

Mann, James. "America's China Fantasy," *American Prospect*, February 19, 2007.

Minqui, Li. "Peak Oil, the Rise of China and India, and the Global Energy Crisis," *Journal of Contemporary Asia*, November 2007.

People's Daily Online. "China Poses No Threat in Post–Cold War World," June 5, 2007. http://english.peopledaily.com.cn/200706/05/eng20070605_380950.html.

Rogge, Jacques, interviewed by Simon Hart. "Olympics: Rogge Backs Beijing over Human Rights," *Telegraph (UK)*, December 3, 2005.

Rosemont Jr., Henry. "Is China a Threat?" *Foreign Policy in Focus*, February 7, 2008. www.fpif.org/fpiftxt/4945.

Schoeman, Maxi. "China in Africa: the Rise of Hegemony?" *Strategic Review for Southern Africa*, November 1, 2007.

Thornton, John L. "Long Time Coming: The Prospects for Democracy in China," *Foreign Affairs*, January/February 2008. www.foreignaffairs.org/20080101faessay87101/john-l-thornton/long-time-coming.html.

Turner, Jennifer L., and Juli S. Kim. "China's Filthiest Export," *Foreign Policy in Focus*, February 7, 2007. www.fpif.org/fpiftxt/3978.

Internet Sources

Feller, Gordon. "China's Renewable Energy: Can Clean Renewables Increase Their Share of China's Rapidly Expanding Energy Sector, and If So, When?" EcoWorld.com, January 31, 2007. www.ecoworld.com/home/articles2.cfm?tid=413.

Jisi, Wang. "China's Road to Peaceful Development and the United States," Real Instituto Elcano, July 27, 2007. www.realinstitutoelcano.org/analisis/ARI2007/ARI90-007_Wang_China_US_Peaceful_Development.pdf.

Kearney, Sally Jean. "China, Tear Down That Great Censorship Wall," Huffington Post.com, July 30, 2008. www.huffingtonpost.com/sally-jean-kearney/china-tear-down-that-grea_b_115955.html.

Lu, Xiaoqing, and Bates Gill. "China's Response to HIV/AIDS and U.S.-China Collaboration," Center for Strategic and International Studies, October 2007. www.csis.org/media/csis/pubs/071002-lu-gill-chinaresponsehiv4web.pdf.

Pan, Esther. "The Scope of China's Military Threat," Council on Foreign Relations, June 2, 2006. www.cfr.org/publication/10824/scope_of_chinas_military_threat.html.

Pei, Minxin. "Corruption Threatens China's Future," Carnegie Endowment for International Peace, October 2007. www.carnegieendowment.org/files/pb55_pei_china_corruption_final.pdf.

Tkacik Jr., John J. "China's Quest for a Superpower Military," Heritage Foundation, Backgrounder No. 2036, May 17, 2007. www.heritage.org/Research/AsiaandthePacific/upload/bg_2036.pdf.

Wortzel, Larry M. "The Chinese People's Liberation Army and Space Warfare: Emerging United States–China Military Competition," American Enterprise Institute, October 17, 2007. www.aei.org/publications/pubID.26977/pub_detail.asp.

Web Sites

AskAsia.com (www.askasia.org). This site, run by the Asia Society, is a helpful and reliable source for students interested in Asian studies, including China.

China Today (www.chinatoday.com). This site contains a wealth of facts, information, articles, pictures, and other information related to life in China.

CIA—The World Factbook—China (www.cia.gov/library/publications/the-world-factbook/geos/ch.html). This page, updated and maintained by the Central Intelligence Agency, contains demographic information on China.

Embassy of People's Republic of China in the United States (www.china-embassy.org/eng). This is the Web site of China's embassy to the United States. Contains numerous links to political and foreign policy topics. The embassy news updates and white papers detail the official Chinese government positions on such issues as Taiwan, China's entry into the World Trade Organization, and human rights. These will be helpful to students looking for primary sources to include in reports.

U.S. Department of State China Homepage (www.state.gov/p/eap/ci/ch/). This site provides reports and news updates on official U.S.-China relations.

The World Bank's China Page (www.worldbank.org/cn). This site is maintained by the World Bank. It offers a country profile on China, links to development reports, and data and statistics on the country.

World Health Organization's China Page (www.who.int/countries/chn/en). Demographics, statistics, and other information on Chinese health issues are found on this page run by the World Health Organization. Students will find numerous statistics and articles for reports.

Index

Picture Credits

Maury Aaseng, 16, 36, 43, 49, 57, 64, 70, 78, 85, 87, 101, 108, 115, 116, 123

AP Images, 69, 76, 98

Zhang Bingtao/Xinhua/Landov, 28

Patty Chen/Reuters/Landov, 41

Claro Cortes IV/Reuters/Landov, 107

David Gray/Reuters/Landov, 13

Reuters/Landov, 47, 113, 120

Toshio Sakai/AFP/Getty Images, 52

Mike Theiler/UPI/Landov, 55

© UpperCut Images/SuperStock, 10

Xinhua/Landov, 22, 34, 80, 83, 91

Bobby Yip/Reuters/Landov, 63

economic integration with China? Levy warns against throwing up our hands on democratic change in China: "The danger is [that] if you rely on . . . those conventional measures, you may reach the erroneous conclusion [that] 'we've achieved nothing through this opening policy, and we'd be more true to ourselves and to our principles if we just shut off trade with China.'" He continues: "Something has happened [there]; you can document it; you can look and see what happened; and we have every reason to think that this has increased the extent to which people's voices are heard—without crossing the threshold."

Signs of Democracy in China

Beijing's Olympics may themselves be a sign of this incipient democracy. The Olympics represent China's wealth, which was driven by the "dual-use" indicators of democratic potential. They are also occasioning flashes of protest within China, a hint of something "incipient" growing just out of sight.

EVALUATING THE AUTHOR'S ARGUMENTS:

The interviewee of this viewpoint, Philip I. Levy, is a researcher with AEI and a former senior trade economist on the President's Council of Economic Advisers. Does knowing the background of this author influence your opinion of his argument? In what way?

Americans Support a Democratic China

Americans favor a number of methods
for promoting democracy in China.

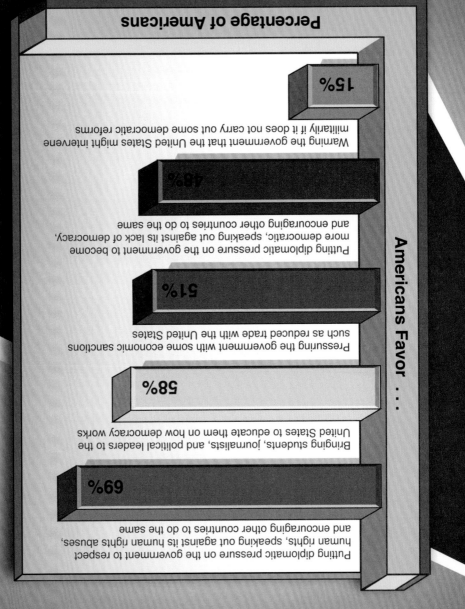

Americans Favor . . .

Percentage of Americans

Putting diplomatic pressure on the government to respect
human rights, speaking out against its human rights abuses,
and encouraging other countries to do the same
69%

Bringing students, journalists, and political leaders to the
United States to educate them on how democracy works
58%

Pressuring the government with some economic sanctions
such as reduced trade with the United States
51%

Putting diplomatic pressure on the government to become
more democratic, speaking out against its lack of democracy,
and encouraging other countries to do the same
48%

Warning the government that the United States might intervene
militarily if it does not carry out some democratic reforms
15%